# Lightworker

# Orientation

# &

# Training

# Manual

# Copyright

**Author:**
Lorelynn Mirage Cardo
www.ariseguide.com

**Book Layout, Interior Design, and Production:**
Cue Raven Publishing
www.cueravenpublishing.com

**Illustrations:**
Kristin Broten
www.kristinbrotenart.com

**Publisher:**
Arise Enterprises, LLC
Lorelynn Mirage Cardo, PhD.

1st Edition

ISBN 13: 978-0-9980113-1-8
ISBN 10: 0-9980113-1-2


Library of Congress:

# *Tools For Lightworkers Series*

Book 1: Daily DeLights Engagement Journal

Book 2: Mandala of Wholeness

Book 3: Prayer of Intent & Guided Visualizations

Book 4: Soul Dialogue: Automatic Writing

Book 5: Lightworker Orientation & Training Manual

Book 6: Reiki 1 & 2 Manual

Book 7: Reiki Master Manual

Book 8: Living Fractals of Light Manual

Book 9: Arise to Soul Psychology

Book 10: Spectrum Energetics: Healing Through Time and Space

Book 11: SoulAnge Harmonics

# Table of Contents

## Part 1 - Energy Matters

### Chapter 1 - Our Personal Energy Management System

### Chapter 2 - Energy Anatomy

### Chapter 3 - Energy Systems

## Part 2 - Energy Healing Work

### Chapter 4 - Energy Tools and Techniques

### Chapter 5 - Energy Trainings

## Chapter 6 - Healing Sessions

### Part 3 - Holding a Mandalic Consciousness:
### Reflections and Feedback

## Chapter 7 - Discerning Sacred Fractal Patterns

### Part 4 - Lightworker, Light Up!

## Chapter 8 - Consciously Create a Lightworker Identity

## Chapter 9 - Quantum Fun and Models of Reality

## Chapter 10 - Mudras and Mantras

## Chapter 11 - Dedication and Service

# Introduction

# Welcome to the
## Arise
## Lightworker Orientation & Training Manual!

Committing yourself to this Apprenticeship is a dedication to your growth as a healer, an empowered energy worker, and a Lightworker. I am honored to walk this path with you and will do everything I can to support you on this journey.

We will be spending much time together over the course of the Apprenticeship and this manual serves as a companion through our journey.

After teaching energy classes for over 20 years, it became apparent that spending a few hours together for class time was not enough time to bathe in the experience, get confident and proficient at skills, and open to all the wonders of being a Lightworker.

To address these concerns, I went back to the basics. Spending more time together over an extended period of time, sharing our sacred stories to see the larger patterns, and practicing our craft – are all time honored techniques of learning and mastering this sacred work.

The Arise Apprenticeship is designed to be a personal, unique journey into the wonder that is You! We will meet regularly in individual guided energy sessions, small group training sessions, and healing technique sessions where we reach out to others in our community.

Throughout our dedicated time together you will be able to expand your personal community of Lightworkers for mutual support. We will also expand our connection with Lightbeings and the Lightworker Grid.

## What is a Lightworker?

Lightworkers are people who are consciously working on being positive, optimistic, and hopeful about themselves, other people, and situations in the world. Lightworkers send love, light, or prayers in times of need. Lightworkers enjoy feeling good and enjoy helping others to feel good too. They see the best in others and learn to see the best in themselves.

## Am I a Lightworker?

If you are reading these words – trust that you are!

My intent through all the years of Arise is to work with those who feel guided to work with me. If you are interested, know that I only work with 'Souls in Service'. These are souls who incarnate with a higher purpose and a higher 'vibratory signature'.

Perhaps you always knew that things were not right in our society, school, work, our environment, or, maybe, in your family. You knew, on a deep level, the importance of being kind and compassionate. Perhaps you wished you were born elsewhere, or maybe not even born at all. Most Lightworkers are very sensitive and feel the harsher and more toxic environments we live in to be daunting.

Nevertheless, this is our conscious soul choice to be here and to shine light so that there may continue an evolution of consciousness. We are part of the story. We are moving the edge of consciousness forward. Trust in yourself and in your destiny path! Most importantly, Lightworkers intend to be grateful for every moment and to live in joy!

Through the Lightworker Orientation and Training Apprenticeship and Manual, may we all know more clearly the joys of being a Lightworker, however that manifests in your life!

## *Lightworker Orientation & Training Apprenticeship:*

There are six levels of training offered. Each level is a year's commitment. You can train for 1 or 2 levels or all 6 levels, based upon your background of energy training.

Using Reiki is a platform energy for all Reiki classes. Reiki 1 and 2 are the introductory levels of training as an energy healer and Lightworker offered at Arise. Reiki Master starts the intermediate level of training.

Karuna Reiki Master ™, and Language of Light™, continue with the intermediate level of energy healer and Lightworker offered at Arise. Karuna is certified through the International Center for Reiki Training. The Language of Light training is offered uniquely at Arise.

Living Fractals of Light™,begins the advanced level of training for energy healer and Lightworker offered uniquely at Arise. This entire series from Reiki 1 through Living Fractals of Light is known as the Reiki Platform.

Spectrum Energetics™, 1 and 2 are both advanced levels of energy healing and Lightworker training, uniquely offered at Arise. It is strongly recommended to study the SoulAnge Reiki Platform before entering into Spectrum Energetics training.

# Six Levels of Training

## Level 1: Lightworker

Offered for those beginning the journey as an energy healer and Lightworker. Reiki 1 and Reiki 2 training is provided which teaches basic hands-on healing and distance healing techniques. Intro to energy healing. Personal empowerment. Chakra balancing and clearing. Boundaries and ethics of sending healings. Beginning energy healing techniques.

## Level 2: Advanced Lightworker

Offered for those who have already received Reiki 1 & 2. Reiki Master will be provided and you will learn to hold mastery energies in your own lives on a daily basis through all situations, personal and global. You will also learn how to teach other students and prepare them to become energy healers. Stand in the world as a master today. Increase your personal empowerment, discernment, and intuitive skills. Intermediate energy healing techniques.

## Level 3: Language of Light Healer

Offered for those who have already received Reiki Master. You will be trained in 2 advanced healing methods. Karuna Reiki Master™ training is provided in accordance to the International Center for Reiki Training. Language of Light Healing Master™ is offered uniquely through Arise and expands further energy systems. Intermediate energy healing techniques.

## Level 4: Advanced Energy Healer

Offered for those who have received Level 3. Sacred geometry, energy glyphs, and expanded chakra systems taught in Living Fractals of Light™ a program taught only at Arise. Includes Christed Light series, Compassionate Light series, Gaia Overlight series, Lightworker Activation series and more. Advanced energy healing techniques.

## Level 5: Etheric Healer

Offered for those who have received levels 3 and 4. You will be trained in an intuitive, etheric healing method: Spectrum Energetics™, a unique chakra based etheric healing method taught exclusively through Arise. Dialogue with guides. Advanced energy healing techniques.

## Level 6: Advanced Etheric Healer

Offered for those who have completed Level 5. Advanced etheric healing methods in SoulAnge Harmonics™. These include angelic lineages and etheric healing models for Hero's Journey, Celebrations, Transitions, Children, Animals, DNA activations, and more. Advanced energy healing techniques.

# Building a Community of Lightworkers

The Apprenticeship is designed to honor those who are meant to be together for the training. Visualize a broadcast being sent out and those who tune into the frequency can hear the message of welcome. Timing, intent, and resonance all play a part.

Your level depends upon your prior energy training. We meet twice a month; once for our main group session and the second time for our energy practice session, Reiki Circle, and Calling All Angels Circle.

Our lives are our textbooks. Our stories and life trajectories are sacred. 'What if' ....everything was really perfect? 'What if'... everything leads to now?

As Lightworkers, we are working multidimensional consciousness and there is no 'higher' or 'lower' status. Everyone is honored for the wisdom, life experience and understandings they bring to the apprenticeship. Level 1 students offer as much of their perspectives as level 6 students.

# Moving River

The Apprenticeship offers a combination of structure, with trainings, tools, techniques and sessions. It is also taught in an organic manner, with topics flowing and changing as the participants evolve. Think of stepping into a moving river. It is the same, and yet it is different. However long you stay with the Apprenticeship, the *Lightworker Orientation and Training Manual* is designed as a layered and guided system. The intent I make for every class is Highest and Greatest Good for All!

We use this Manual as a guide and each year will be unique because we continually grow and evolve. We may get to most areas each year, and you may work on some areas during your personal session. There is a balance of new, advanced, and unique exercises and perspectives as this Apprenticeship and Manual comes from my background, life experience and unique outlook.We spiral through these learnings at different levels each and every time.

# Partnership in Training

A second way we work through the Apprenticeship as a moving river is that each group is unique and we partner together in terms of covering material. Some groups are very interested in esoteric information, others in energy tools, healing sessions, or in developing self-confidence as a healer and Lightworker. Therefore, each group training session is uniquely designed for the individuals in the group and their specific needs and interests.

Trust that you are pulling in the information you need and want. Each Apprentice year is unique because you, and your group, are unique.

This winding pathway parallels the adage that you can never step into the same river twice. It is a moving, organic journey. It is a partnership of learning, growing, and broadcasting together.

# Certifications

If you are a beginner, you will be taught Reiki 1 and 2. However, this Apprenticeship is not 'just' a Reiki class or a Reiki Apprenticeship. This is a Lightworker Apprenticeship, and Reiki is a foundation. Reiki is guided and is taught by an attunement method, so it is easily accessible for all. Reiki has been a foundational platform in my life and work, and I teach from this perspective.

'Rei' is a Japanese word meaning consciousness, intelligent universal life force, or God's power. 'Ki' relates to our personal energy system. It is a merging of the individual with the divine. 'Reiki' means spiritually guided life force energy.

At the successful completion of the year program you will receive an Arise Lightworker certificate, beginner, intermediate or advanced, depending upon your level of training.

Reiki 1, 2, and Master levels are Usui certified and you will receive a certified Reiki practitioner certificate which can be used for CEU credits, for registration with many volunteer programs in hospitals and hospice centers, for giving healing sessions and, if Master, train others in Reiki worldwide. Karuna Reiki Master™ is certified through the International Center for Reiki Training and upon successful completion you will receive a Center certificate with an identifying number which allows you to teach Karuna Reiki™ worldwide.

The advanced level trainings are all uniquely offered only at Arise and you will receive certificates for Language of Light Healer™, Living Fractal of Light Healing Mastery™, Spectrum Energetics Etheric Healer™, and SoulAnge Harmonics Advanced Etheric Healer™. For these advanced healing trainings you will be able to teach and attune others in these methods.

# Entrance Considerations

## Interest in Energy Healing:

You should have an interest in energy healing and an openness for personal growth and introspection. Much of our work is sharing and discovery, as the universal fractal is repeated in each of our lives. There are appropriate levels and boundaries to disclosure. No one need feel pressured to share, and the environment is one of respect, appreciation, support, safety and celebration.

## Flexible models of reality:

Our willingness to grow and be challenged equals our willingness to respectfully listen and consider other points of view. It's good to have flexible models of reality as we will circling around your core beliefs and you might encounter stories from others of different models of reality. We all believe our version is the right one, but, as our scientists and metaphysicians remind us, we are vibrational interpreters and much of our perception is unique.

## Ethics:

High ethical and integrity codes are critical in energy work especially as we are in each other's fields and can access much personal and soul information. It is so important to refine our discerning abilities between true intuition, guided information, imagination, and best guesses based on our experiences.

## Receptive:

As you are Apprenticing to me, it is important that you are receptive to my lead and my perspective. I honor each person's path and always reach for the pristine quality of having no agenda for you personally, except

*"I honor your unique soul path, your free will choices, and the Highest and Greatest Good".*

I see myself as a guide who has traversed some of the terrain you are now traveling, otherwise you would not be guided to work with me. That doesn't mean you need to follow in my footsteps, or follow a path I might point out to you. But I ask that you are receptive to my direction.

## Commitment:

There should be a commitment to coming to the meetings and finishing the yearly program. There are bi-monthly group sessions on specific trainings and energy techniques. You will also be asked for an investment of time and energy to read and complete exercises every month.

This is all about honoring you, your time, and your ability to move at your perfect pace. This is not a 'school' environment.

## Meetings:

The more you commit to the program for the year, the more you will enjoy it and get the most out of it. We meet regularly – plan to schedule other activities, when possible, around our meeting times. You are asked to reflect on both our meetings and our energy sessions, so you can capture and reflect back upon the information at later times.

We also meet for a monthly personal session. This is your time. Normally, we check in for the pattern or issue you would like to discuss and then enjoy a personal energy session. Some months, there is much guided work for you to consider. Other times, we might solely engage in energy work on the table. Again, whatever is perfect for you at your time is appropriate. You are asked to reflect on our personal sessions and your 'homework', so you can capture and reflect back upon the information at later times.

Remember, every aspect of the program is layered. We work with fractals of wholeness! Finally, it's important to enjoy a good laugh – even if it is at ourselves.

# *Lightworker Manual Overview*

There are 4 main parts to the *Lightworker Orientation & Training Manual*. Each area engages you with a series of open-ended questions and reflections. There are summary areas at the end of each chapter and the end of the entire section.

Within all the sections, there are multiple spaces for note taking, reflections, coloring, doodling, and giving the manual your own personal journalistic, artistic and heartfelt touches.

Below is a quick glance at the four major areas.

## Part 1: Energy Matters

The first section provides light monitoring of your personal energy management system, including physical, emotional, mental and spiritual/energetic components. Additional areas cover energy anatomy (aura, chakras, intuition and higher gifts) and energy systems, or a look at various engines that drive incarnation from energy into matter.

## Part 2: Energy Training

This second part details a number of energy tools which will be covered extensively in our group meetings. Some tools are more general and can easily be used by all. Others are more specific and require your discernment about use.

There is space provided for reflections on the attunements, and class notes. Summaries of preparing for, conducting, clearing and ending a healing session are provided with quick check-lists provided.

## Part 3: Holding a Mandalic Consciousness: Reflections & Feedback

Part 3 invites you to reflect upon the various ways you are interacting in the Apprenticeship. Each component is an integral part of the whole of your Mandalic Consciousness. Patterns in one area might easily be found again in other areas of your life. These repeating patterns are known as 'fractals'. As we take responsibility and heal our wounded fractal patterns, our consciousness enlightens and enlifts as well.

There are multiple worksheets within this area including reflections and feedback on 30 client/healing sessions and feedback from partnering and sending Reiki throughout the year.

There are also worksheets for you to reflect upon including our monthly group Apprentice sessions, monthly personal sessions, intuition partnering, Lightworker group sending sessions, energy boosts and seasonal intents.

## Part 4: Lightworker, Light Up!

This final part covers qualities and perspectives helpful for consciously creating a Lightworker identity. We briefly touch upon quantum healing theory and practices. You are gifted with your unique SoulAnge Harmonics or angelic lineage and attributes. You are also encouraged to create or channel a melody to sing in your name and lineage, and we can sing it in for you!

The last chapter is devoted to professionalizing your work and broadcasting your Lightwork out into the world.

# Distance Training

This Manual can be used in conjunction with a distance Apprenticeship for those who don't live in the Portland, Oregon local area.

We can cover the training by phone or Skype. You will need to be present on-site at least once in the year for the actual training and attuning classes,

- Reiki 1and Reiki 2 training is 1 day each.
- Reiki Master requires 2 days.
- All the advanced classes require 3 - 4 days of training.

# Supplemental Materials and the Tools for Lightworkers Series

In addition to the *Lightworker Orientation & Training Manual*, additional supplemental materials will be provided throughout the training.

This Manual is Book 5 of the *Arise Tools for Lightworkers* series. We will also be working with Books 1 - 4 for the Apprenticeship.

Book 1, *Daily DeLights Engagement Journal* will help us anchor in and light up every day. Daily DeLights is designed to integrate with Part 1 of this Manual, Honoring Our Vehicle, as we work with our personal energy management system and align through our physical, emotional, mental and spiritual/energetic fields.

Book 2, *Mandala of Wholeness*, Companion & Compendium to *Daily DeLights*, is a more detailed look at the GRACE! process outlined in Daily DeLights. There are 13 mandalas to meditate upon as we focus upon lighting up our physical, emotional, mental, spiritual/energetic fields through the four seasons. We bring conscious intent while incarnating through our days and ensouling through our nights. The final mandala brings us back to wholeness.

Book 3, *Prayers of Intent & Guided Visualizations* offers step-by-step instruction on designing your prayers of intent and presents many examples of setting intent and working with clients on guided visualizations for healing sessions, energy classes, and attunements. Feeling comfortable verbalizing our, and our client's, intents is important in energy healing. It is also important for professional ethics and assuring we have protections in place and being agenda free.

Book 4, *Soul Dialogues through Automatic Writing*, offers step-by-step instruction on automatic writing, a practice which increases intuitive skills. There is ample space to practice and samples of soul dialogues.

Each of these four books will add to our knowledge base and will give you many tools for your energy healing and Lightwork.

# Advanced Teachings and the Tools for Lightworkers Series

Books 6 and 7 are detailed manuals for teaching and attuning others for *Reiki 1 & 2* (Book 6) and *Reiki Master* (Book 7). These are Usui Reiki manuals and prepare Reiki Masters to teach classes to interested students.

Book 8, *Living Fractals of Light*, is a manual for teaching and attuning others in advanced energy healing. It is designed for those who have completed Reiki Master and Karuna Reiki Master™. Living Fractals of Light™ is a unique sound and energy glyph, highly intuitive healing method taught only at Arise. A true language of light, the Living Fractals are dimensional doorways that allow us to step through and bring sound healing and sacred geometries into our lives and our healing practice.

*Arise: Soul Based Perspectives on Counseling and Healing*, Book 9, is a detailed discussion of pioneering theory and practice in the counseling and mental health fields. It is designed for both those in the field as well as others who are interested in attaining self- actualization, self-awareness, and holding a larger identity perspective outside of traditional counseling and mental health paradigms.

*Spectrum Energetics: Etheric and Chakra Healings Through Time, Space and Dimension*, Book 10, is a detailed discussion of etheric healing. Spectrum Energetics ™ is a unique chakra based healing method taught only at Arise.

*SoulAnge Harmonic Angelic Lineages*, Book 11, details soul and angelic names and their lineages direct from Source. Harmonic Angelic Lineages™ is a unique system taught only at Arise.

# A Note from Lorelynn

*If you are guided to work with me, trust that you are a Lightworker and a Soul in Service!*

*The Lightworker Orientation and Training Manual serves as an inspiration, guide, and personal note-taking tool. Write as much or as little as you like. Share with me or with our group those parts you feel comfortable sharing. You can be assured that this is a private window into your world at this moment in time.*
*Relax, grab a pen or markers, a cup of tea, and begin!*
*Let's enJoy our precious time together!*

# Pre-Apprentice Check-In

The following check-in will help you gauge your pre-Apprentice understandings.

Date:_____

Do you identify yourself as a Lightworker?

_____

_____

_____

Do you identify yourself as an Energy Worker?

_____

_____

_____

How else do you identify yourself?

_____

_____

_____

What does it mean to be a Lightworker?

_____

_____

_____

_____

_____

What do you want to get from this Apprenticeship?

_____

_____

_____

_____

_____

_____

Are you happy with your daily alignment? Anything you would like to be different?

_____

_____

_____

_____

_____

What are some of your self-care tools?

_____

_____

_____

Do you send energy every day for the Highest and Greatest Good for situations?

_____

_____

Do you have intuitive gifts?  Please explain.

_____

_____

_____

_____

_____

_____

_____

What is the highest vision you hold for yourself?

_____

_____

_____

_____

_____

To feel successful, what goals do you have by the end of the Arise Apprenticeship?

_____

_____

_____

_____

_____

Other Notes:

_____

_____

_____

_____

_____

_____

_____

_____

_____

_____

_____

_____

_____

_____

_____

_____

_____

_____

# *Introduction*

## Energy Does Matter!  We Matter!

In Part 1, *Energy Matters*, we start with an overview of energy dynamics. Energy does matter.  And energy becomes matter - as us, the reality and beauty of being in human form.

Mystics, saints, and now physicists, the metaphysicians of our time, tell us the same origin story. We are energy made flesh. We are special. And, we are truly made of stardust. The elements which make up our bodies are the result of star systems, supernovas, imploding, exploding and sending carbon and other heavy elements outward across the universe. Energy and matter dance across the face of the cosmos for billions and billions of years and we are in the unique position to bring our conscious awareness into this origin story of energy becoming individualized units of matter.

**Chapter 1, Your Personal Energy Management System**, looks at the component parts of our total human energy system. You will have an opportunity to monitor your body (physical system), your guidance (emotional and mental systems), and your highest guidance (spiritual and energetic systems).

This part ends with an overview of *Daily DeLights, an Engagement Journal for Lightworkers*, Book 1 of the *Tools for Lightworkers Series*. This engagement journal is a day by day process for aligning and centering ourselves so that we can light up our lives.

**Chapter 2, Energy Anatomy**, delves deeper into our energy systems or how energy transduces into human form. We look at various underlying structures including soul contracts, chakras, intuitive abilities, lightbody and ascension, and ways of continuing the dialogue with non-physical awareness.

**Chapter 3, Energy Systems**, is an overview of various layers of consciousness, universal laws, and exercises designed to enable us to synch more effectively and joyfully into our partnership of spirit and physical form. A running joke is that it is unfortunate that we don't come with manuals. The truth is, we do! But the fun and challenge is to correctly interpret the instructional manual, follow the directions, and then ... have fun!

# Part 1

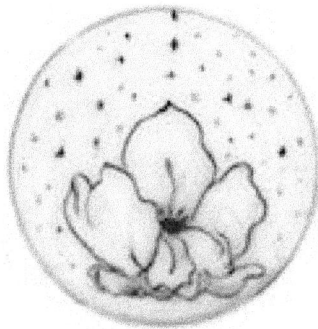

# Energy Matters

# Chapter 1

# Our Personal

# Energy

# Management System

# (PEMS)

# Our Personal Energy Management System

The acronym PEMS commonly stands for physical, emotional, mental and spiritual areas. For us, PEMS also stands for our personal energy management system. As Lightworkers, it is important to be aware of all our systems and work to keep them all in alignment with each other.

It is our responsibility to manage our fields and be in joy and harmony. As Lightworkers it is our ability and our responsibility to work every day to align ourselves so that we may do our work: sending Light to ourselves, our loved ones, our communities, and our world.

It is hard to do our work when we are distracted by internal storms of pain and confusion.

We are taught many things in our schools especially how to read, write, and logically think. Since our earliest years, educational Institutions have control over our time, our social connections, our internal tapes of how smart and creative we are, and our files of all sorts of data, much of it trivial. But we are not taught how to monitor, adjust, and excel with our internal physical, emotional, mental and spiritual/energetic fields.

Visualize how interesting a system of learning that would be!

We would have time to get to know and work with our bodies and learn how to ground ourselves. We would have time to follow pursuits that interest and challenge us emotionally, mentally, and creatively. We would probably be outdoors much more, and certainly not so sedentary. And, of course, we would be more inner directed and not so controlled by an expert who follows a fairly rigid system that may or may not meet our needs and our interests.

We would be more in line with our inner selves, those soft whispers that call to us from time to time.

Can you remember early school years, before you were 'socialized' into the institution so tightly that you didn't feel resistance? I can clearly remember looking out windows at a beautiful day, looking at the slowly turning clock, and wishing with all my heart that we could be outdoors. Even if it were sitting outside learning material that made no sense to memorize. Just to feel the breeze on my face, or the sun, or even snow and rain. But due to constraints of teaching large groups of students large amounts of information, we were socialized away from feeling our natural thirst, hunger, boredom, creative daydreaming, the need to move, run, or feel free.

Compound that by 12 years, 16 years, or more, and we find ourselves in a society that moves relentlessly from early school training to full life/ full time work entraining. There is little time to touch base with ourselves physically, emotionally, mentally and spiritually/energetically.

Therefore, in this first section, we take the time to check in with all our systems. You are asked to reflect upon a number of prompts which will take you through your current awareness of your personal energy management systems.

# Chapter 1 Overview

This first chapter on personal energy management, covers the three PEMS areas: physical, mental/emotional and spiritual/energetic. You are invited through a number of prompts to get a snapshot of your fields and how you manage them. Each section also has a summary and affirmations page.

Section 1 is a short overview of the physical field. In this section you will consider your bodily awareness, sleep, energy levels, and nature activities.

Many Lightworkers are not well grounded. We enjoy the inner world so much that it is hard to be in physical. Also, many Lightworkers have come from a 'wounded healer path', experiencing much pain and trauma through early years. As we heal ourselves, we set healing markers for others to follow as well. However, there are side effects of walking the wounded healer path including shredded boundaries, oversensitivity, hypervigilance, and disassociation from physical senses.

Therefore, grounding and rooting may not feel so natural for you. But it is our platform to be in our biology and to build our canopies from that grounded and rooted place.

Section 2 is an overview of your mental and emotional fields including your emotional landscape, family patterns, self-reflections on your brilliance, passions, dreams, personality, and deep longings. This short overview can give you a good understanding of how aligned and centered you are on a daily basis.

Section 3 offers an opportunity for you to consider for your spiritual and energy fields including your inner world, inner connections, energy tools and trainings, boundaries, and sacred contracts. This chapter can offer you a glimpse into your ability to elevate above cause and effect and your ability to breathe compassionate action into your life.

Section 4 is a short overview of two other books in the Tools for Lightworkers Series: *Daily DeLights Engagement Journal for Lightworkers,* and *The Mandala of Wholeness*. These two supplemental materials help to bring daily consciousness to our personal energy management systems.

EnJoy this quick review of your physical, emotional, mental, and spiritual/energetic bodies. The clearer and more defined our earthwalk, the stronger and more refined our Lightwork!

# Section 1

## *Honoring Our Vehicle*

## Monitoring our Physical Body

Let's start at the beginning!  The way upward is by anchoring firmly within our biology. This first chapter focuses on our physical body, encouraging us to ground and root.

## Eating habits and food

1. Please take a few moments to describe how your eating habits have developed. How happy are you with your food choices?  How does your body feel after eating?

_____

_____

_____

_____

_____

_____

_____

_____

_____

_____

_____

_____

2.  Think about your earliest memories with food – who cooked for you?  What foods did you like? Did you feel sick after eating? What 'food rules' were there in your early home (clean your plate, etc.)?  Was family eating a nurturing or stressful experience?

_____

_____

_____

_____

_____

_____

_____

_____

_____

_____

_____

_____

_____

_____

_____

_____

3. What would you like to change about your food and/or your eating habits?

_____

_____

_____

_____

_____

_____

4. What types of things have you tried in the past?

_____

_____

_____

_____

_____

_____

_____

5. How confident are you that you can make lasting changes if you need to or want to?

_____

_____

_____

6.  What ideal goals do you hold about food, eating habits, and weight?

_____

_____

_____

_____

_____

_____

7.  What goals would be wonderful for you <u>right now</u>?

_____

_____

_____

_____

_____

## Sleep

8.  When do you go to bed? When do you wake up? Do you follow an inner rhythm or a clock? How is your sleep (deep, restful, interrupted, etc.)?

_____

_____

_____

_____

_____

9. What have you tried in the past to help with any sleep issues (if you have any)? How was sleeping when you were younger?

_____

_____

_____

_____

_____

_____

_____

10. Are you refreshed when you wake up?

_____

_____

_____

_____

11. Is there anything you would like to change about your sleep?

_____

_____

_____

_____

_____

_____

_____

12. What are your ideal goals about sleep?

_____

_____

_____

_____

_____

_____

_____

13. What is a wonderful goal for you to hold for yourself <u>right now</u>?

_____

_____

_____

_____

_____

_____

_____

## Moving your body

14. What are your favorite ways to move?

_____

_____

_____

_____

15. What things have you done in the past?

_____

_____

_____

_____

_____

16. What can you visualize yourself doing?  (hiking, skydiving, mountain climbing, running,,,,,)

_____

_____

_____

_____

17. How do people in your family move?  What were messages about exercising when you were young, at home, and in school?

_____

_____

_____

_____

_____

_____

18. What are your ideal goals about moving your body?

_____

_____

_____

_____

_____

_____

19. What is a great way for you to move your body <u>right now</u>?

_____

_____

_____

_____

## Body care and body awareness

20. Have you made friends with your body? Do you admire and appreciate all your varying parts?

_____

_____

_____

_____

_____

_____

21. Do you enjoy caring for your body?

_____

_____

_____

_____

_____

_____

22. Do you have special body related rituals for waking up and going to sleep? Any ways you would like to increase or shift them?

_____

_____

_____

_____

_____

23. Are there parts of your body that you are not happy with? How can you make peace/ friends with these areas (if any)?

_____

_____

_____

_____

_____

24. Think back to your childhood and teenage years.  How did you view your body when you were younger?  Did you enjoy caring for your body in earlier years?

_____

_____

_____

_____

_____

25. How did your family members view caring for their bodies?

_____

_____

_____

_____

_____

26. What ideal goals do you have about body care and body awareness?

_____

_____

_____

_____

_____

_____

27. What is an easy, effortless goal to hold for your body care <u>right now</u>?

_____

_____

_____

_____

_____

## Energy levels

28. Do you recognize peaks and valleys in energy levels during your days and nights?

_____

_____

_____

_____

_____

29. Are you fatigued during the day?  If so, when?

_____

_____

_____

_____

_____

_____

30. What do you do with your peaks and valleys?

_____

_____

_____

_____

_____

31. How do you work with your energy levels?  (Ex. get more energy from coffee; sleep with an herbal supplement?)

_____

_____

_____

_____

_____

32. Did you always have the same energy levels as you do today?

_____

_____

_____

_____

_____

33. What is a good goal for you <u>right now</u>?

_____

_____

_____

_____

_____

## Nature

34. Do you enjoy being in nature?  What types of ways are you in nature?

_____

_____

_____

_____

_____

_____

35. What ideal visions and goals do you hold about being in nature?

_____

_____

_____

_____

_____

36. Do you walk the land regularly?

_____

_____

_____

_____

_____

37. Do you work with nature's gifts?  (rocks, crystals, plants)

_____

_____

_____

_____

_____

_____

38. Do you have a safe, serene nature-based place that you love and feel safe in?

_____

_____

_____

_____

_____

_____

39. Do you enjoy working with animal companions?

_____

_____

_____

_____

_____

40. Are you aligned with any special animals or have had animals visit you in dreams? Which ones?

_____

_____

_____

_____

_____

_____

41. Do you work with oils, flower essences, gemstones, elixirs? If not, are you interested in doing so?

_____

_____

_____

_____

_____

_____

42. What is an attainable way for you to be in nature <u>right now</u>?

_____

_____

_____

_____

## Overall health and rejuvenation

43. How would you describe your overall health? Are you at ease or in dis-ease?

_____

_____

_____

_____

_____

_____

44. What long range goals do you hold about your health and rejuvenation?

_____

_____

_____

_____

_____

_____

45. How do you view aging?

_____

_____

_____

_____

_____

_____

46. Are there things you could do to rejuvenate yourself?  What have you tried?

_____

_____

_____

_____

_____

_____

47. What one thing could you do to increase your overall health and vitality <u>right now</u>?

_____

_____

_____

_____

_____

48. What one thing could you do to rejuvenate yourself <u>right now</u>?

_____

_____

_____

_____

_____

_____

## *Summary Reflections*

# Invest time to review *Honoring your Physical Vehicle*

Do you see any patterns?  Are you ready to release any negative thoughts, memories, perceptions, behaviors, or habits you might be holding that is not respecting your body? Are you escaping with addictions and wish to move beyond these stuck routines? While holding a vision of ideal goals, what ones could you effortlessly and joyfully bring into your life <u>right now</u>?

_____

_____

_____

_____

_____

_____

_____

_____

_____

_____

_____

_____

_____

# *Affirmations*

Write, sing, draw, dance some affirmations to honor your magnificent body, your organs and systems, being in physical form, and enjoying incarnating and experiencing life through an individual lens of consciousness!

_____

_____

_____

_____

_____

_____

_____

_____

_____

_____

_____

_____

_____

_____

_____

_____

# Section 2

## *Honoring Our Guidance Systems*

## Monitoring our Emotional and Mental Bodies

This chapter focus our attention on our inner perceptions and worlds, encouraging us to align and center.

### Emotional Landscape

1. Let's focus on your emotions. Describe your basic personality type and how you live within the ocean of emotion.

_____

_____

_____

_____

_____

_____

_____

_____

_____

_____

_____

_____

_____

2.  Is there anything you wish to change in your emotional landscape (heighten, lessen, etc.)?

_____

_____

_____

_____

_____

_____

_____

_____

3.  Are you familiar with the Abraham-Hicks Emotional Guidance Scale? If yes, have you worked your way to levels 1 -6?  What do you think of this Scale?

_____

_____

_____

_____

_____

_____

_____

_____

4.  One fascinating perspective of the Emotional Guidance Scale is that we have a range that cycles around a "vibrational set point." Do you have a vibrational set point? What is your common daily range?

_____

_____

_____

_____

_____

_____

_____

5.  How were emotions handled in your family? Do you see patterns in your own life and relationships?

_____

_____

_____

_____

_____

_____

_____

_____

_____

_____

*Arise Lightworker Orientation and Training Manual*

## Mental Brilliance

6. How mentally brilliant do you think you are?  How brilliant at surviving and thriving were your family of origin?  Did you like school?  Did you succeed within that system?  Start at kindergarten and move your way up...

## Pre-K and Kindergarten

_____

_____

1st
_____

_____

2nd
_____

_____

3rd
_____

_____

4th
_____

_____

5th
_____

_____

6th
_____

_____

7th
_____

_____

48

8th

_____

_____

High School Freshman

_____

_____

High School Sophomore

_____

_____

High School Junior

_____

_____

High School Senior

_____

_____

Higher Education

_____

_____

_____

Multiple Intelligence theory lists up to 9 types of intelligences. These range from the two basic ones taught and tested in schools: verbal and logical/mathematical.

## Other intelligences, according to Howard Gardner, are:

- Kinesthetic (body),
- visual-spatial,
- interpersonal (social),
- intrapersonal (inner awareness),
- musical,
- naturalist (environment), and perhaps
- moral and spiritual.

7. What are your highest intelligences and modes of learning? Where they honored throughout your life and schooling?

_____

_____

_____

_____

_____

_____

_____

_____

_____

_____

_____

_____

Have you considered a personality/Jung typology quick assessment?  Try
www.humanmetrics.com to see how you score on:

- Introversion/extraversion
- Intuition/sensing
- Thinking/feeling
- Perceiving/judging

8.   Does this add to your understanding of your unique personality?

_____

_____

_____

_____

_____

_____

_____

9.   What are some of your more endearing, even if quirky, characteristics?

_____

_____

_____

_____

_____

_____

_____

_____

10. What are some of your passions – some that have been with you from earliest memories and some that keep coming to mind even now?

_____

_____

_____

_____

_____

_____

_____

11. What do you do to bring your emotions and thoughts to a higher level during the day or at night?

_____

_____

_____

_____

_____

_____

_____

_____

_____

## Dreams

Dreams serve a number of purposes. They are a good way to decompress from our day. Other times dreams help us work on daily issues or problems. Sometimes dreams are actual portals to other realms or dimensions and we can receive guidance from them.

Before you go to bed one night, set the intent that you will access higher guidance (in general or for a specific area of your life). And affirm that you will remember your dream.

12. Share a dream that conveyed to you important information or messages.

_____

_____

_____

_____

_____

_____

_____

_____

_____

_____

_____

_____

_____

_____

_____

13. Share a dream that opened up new portals or multidimensional states (ex. flying, etc.)

_____

_____

_____

_____

_____

_____

_____

_____

_____

_____

_____

_____

_____

_____

_____

_____

_____

_____

14. Share a dream in which you were able to see and speak to Loved Ones who transitioned.

_____

_____

_____

_____

_____

_____

_____

_____

_____

_____

_____

_____

_____

_____

_____

_____

_____

_____

## Fears

We all have fears – personal, generational, familial (through our DNA), cellular, ancestral, and through the collective conscious and unconscious to our culture and to the entire global community.

That's a lot of fear!  What are some of your fears?  Your greatest fear? A recurring fear?

For those of us on the Lightworker path, we look at, and work with our fears. We remember all is well, all is well, all is always well, even in our perfect imperfection.

As Lightworkers, when we heal an area of fear within ourselves, we set healings to all others who are wrestling with that particular fear.

15. Expand your vision of why we face fears and how we help others to move beyond them.

_____

_____

_____

_____

_____

_____

_____

_____

_____

_____

## Career Trajectories

16. Reflect on your earliest jobs and list them all!  Have fun!  Include part time, full time, and volunteer.

_____

_____

_____

_____

_____

_____

_____

_____

_____

_____

_____

_____

_____

_____

_____

_____

_____

17. Are you surprised at this list of all your work related activities?

_____

_____

_____

_____

_____

_____

18. Do you notice any recurring patterns in your work life?

_____

_____

_____

_____

_____

19. How do you feel about your work life as it has woven throughout your life?

_____

_____

_____

_____

_____

_____

20. Do you have yearning for other work life experiences?  What are they?

_____

_____

_____

_____

_____

_____

_____

_____

## Highest and Greatest Visions

It is easy to succumb to thoughts of scarcity, lack, greed, conspiracy, and all other denser vibrations because we swim in a sea of those emotions.  As Lightworkers, we learn to reach for, hold the vibration of, and intend 'Highest and Greatest Good for All'!

21. Dystopic, or doom-and-gloom stories, movies, talk surround us. Instead, what visions can we create that are filled with hope, light, optimism, community, sustainability, compassion...?

_____

_____

_____

_____

_____

_____

22. What are the highest visions you hold for yourself?

_____

_____

_____

_____

_____

_____

_____

_____

_____

_____

_____

_____

_____

_____

_____

_____

_____

_____

_____

23. What are the highest visions you hold for all of us on Earth?

_____

_____

_____

_____

_____

_____

_____

_____

_____

_____

_____

_____

_____

_____

_____

_____

_____

_____

_____

# *Summary Reflections*

Take a little time to review Loving Our Higher Guidance Systems of mental and emotional states.

Do you see any patterns? Are you ready to release any negative thoughts, memories, perceptions, behaviors, or habits you might be holding that is not respecting your emotional states and mental abilities? Are you escaping with addictions and wish to move beyond these stuck routines? While holding a vision of ideal goals, what ones could you effortlessly and joyfully bring into your life <u>right now</u>?

_____

_____

_____

_____

_____

_____

_____

_____

_____

_____

_____

_____

_____

_____

_____

# *Affirmations*

Write, sing, draw, dance some affirmations to honor your higher guidance systems of perceiving and enjoying your emotions and of recognizing and allowing for your mental genius and unique, wonderful personality!

_____

_____

_____

_____

_____

_____

_____

_____

_____

_____

_____

_____

_____

_____

_____

# Section 3

## *Honoring Our Highest and Greatest Partner*

## Monitoring our Spiritual and Energetic Bodies

We are not humans with a soul.  We are magnificent, eternal, powerful creators of Love and Light who have chosen to participate in this Grand Adventure!

We are Love and we are Loved. We are honorable and we are honored.

1.  If you have a **spiritual practice**, please share it here.  What is it? How do you connect? How often? How is it working for you?

_____

_____

_____

_____

_____

_____

_____

_____

_____

_____

_____

_____

_____

2.  What does 'spirituality' mean to you?  What does 'religion' mean to you?

_____

_____

_____

_____

_____

_____

_____

_____

_____

_____

_____

_____

_____

_____

_____

_____

_____

_____

3.  What are your earliest remembrances of connection with Spirit (God, Universe, Creator)? What path were you set on as a child? How have you navigated through that particular causeway?

_____

_____

_____

_____

_____

_____

_____

_____

_____

_____

_____

_____

_____

_____

_____

_____

_____

_____

4. How is your inner world populated?  Do you dialogue or pray to particular Ascended Loving Beings?

_____

_____

_____

_____

_____

_____

_____

_____

_____

_____

_____

_____

_____

_____

_____

_____

_____

_____

_____

5. How do you discern the differences between mental survival tapes, gut instinct, intuition, and higher guidance?

_____

_____

_____

_____

_____

_____

_____

_____

_____

_____

_____

_____

_____

_____

_____

_____

_____

_____

6. Do you currently practice energy techniques?  Which ones?  Why were you drawn to them?

_____

_____

_____

_____

_____

_____

_____

_____

7. Do you pray or send energy healings to others every day? Would you want to?

_____

_____

_____

_____

_____

_____

_____

_____

8. List each chakra and what you know about each. Do you work on clearing and balancing your chakras frequently?

_____

_____

_____

_____

_____

_____

_____

_____

_____

_____

_____

_____

_____

_____

_____

_____

_____

_____

9. Do you set **boundaries**, protections and conditions around yourself, your home, work, car?

_____

_____

_____

_____

_____

_____

_____

_____

_____

10. Do you feel safe from unwanted influences?

_____

_____

_____

_____

_____

_____

_____

_____

_____

11. What does **forgiveness** mean to you?

_____

_____

_____

_____

_____

_____

_____

12. Do you need to forgive yourself for anything you have said or done or thought?

_____

_____

_____

_____

_____

_____

_____

_____

_____

_____

13. Are there people you need to forgive?

_____

_____

_____

_____

_____

_____

_____

14. How does your **creativity** manifest in your life?   How would you like it to?

_____

_____

_____

_____

_____

_____

_____

_____

_____

15. If you could be any type of artist, what kind would you choose today?  Why?

_____

_____

_____

_____

_____

_____

_____

_____

_____

_____

_____

_____

_____

_____

_____

_____

_____

_____

Consider the Sacred Contracts you have made with everyone in your life up until this time (!)

16. Do you see any patterns? Are you unsure why another person or situation is in your life?

_____

_____

_____

_____

_____

_____

_____

_____

_____

_____

_____

_____

_____

_____

_____

_____

17. Consider and be creative with soul contracts with each person in your family of origin and move to your nuclear and extended families, friends, and expand outward.

_____

_____

_____

_____

_____

_____

_____

_____

_____

_____

_____

_____

_____

_____

_____

_____

_____

18. How do you practice compassion –in-action?

_____

_____

_____

_____

_____

_____

_____

_____

_____

_____

_____

_____

_____

_____

_____

_____

_____

# Summary Reflections

Take a little time to review *Honoring Our Highest Guidance and Spiritual Selves.*

Are there any longings or aspirations you hold for yourself in this sacred area?

_____

_____

_____

_____

_____

_____

_____

_____

_____

_____

_____

_____

_____

_____

_____

# *Affirmations*

Write, sing, draw, dance some affirmations to connect more fully with the inner dimensions and prayers of the heart!

_____

_____

_____

_____

_____

_____

_____

_____

_____

_____

_____

_____

_____

_____

_____

_____

# Section 4

## *Daily DeLights and*

## *The Mandala of Wholeness*

### Books 1 and 2 of the
### Tools For Lightworkers Series

*Daily DeLights* and the *Mandala of Wholeness* are two supplementary books which offer two related yet unique perspectives on our personal energy management system (PEMS).

## Daily DeLights

*Daily DeLights* is a perpetual annual calendar which helps chart our energy systems. Book 1 of the *Tools for Lightworkers Series*, *Daily DeLights* is seasonally based so we can honor our Earth partnership and move with the pulse of the seasons.

You can start any day of the year. January 1st is a wonderful, mostly global, perspective on annual cycles, but we are not bound by the convention. Many peoples have honored spring equinox as a beginning cycle, or full moons. Perhaps we like to measure from our birthdays. Sometimes we begin when we need to begin. *Daily DeLights* honors your timing.

There are two unique elements to the *Daily DeLights* model: the *GRACE!* process and the *Solar Grid*. With these models we effortlessly monitor our personal energy management system, chart our progress, and become our own best friend.

# GRACE!

*GRACE!* stands for:

- Grounding
- Rooting
- Aligning
- Centering
- Elevating
- (Alchemical pop)!

Grounding and rooting refer to our physical and familial systems

Aligning and centering refer to our mental and emotional systems

Elevating and allowing for the alchemical pop (!) refer to our spiritual and energetic systems

Together the *GRACE!* process and *Daily DeLights* help us to light up every day. By choosing an activity to highlight each of the fundamental areas, we balance our lives and our life purpose. A good analogy is a strand of lights. When one part goes out, the whole strand stops shining. As Lightworkers, we, too, need to be in alignment on all our levels or we risk burning out from overstraining in one area, neglecting another.

Time is not a restriction or boundary. All six activities can be accomplished in less than a minute. We make our best effort to allow *GRACE!* to fill our lives.

# The Mandala of Wholeness

Book 2 of the *Tools for Lightworkers Series, The Mandala of Wholeness* is a compendium and companion to *Daily DeLights*. It offers many examples of activites for each of the *GRACE!* areas through all the seasons, and for day time joys and night time ensoulment.

Each of these areas are viewed through the lens of a mandala and we are encouraged to create our own mandala of wholeness for our unique journey. There are 13 mandalas in all, each contributing a fractal design of the whole, similar to nature's abundant and magnificent fractal designs.

In the *Mandala of Wholeness* we view our life from a larger, more expansive perspective. The whole is always more than the sum of the parts of our lives.

It is our responsibility to shine our light and to align ourselves, balance, enjoy the process so our light is not filtered through personal pain, desperation, or an over exaggerated need to 'help' others.

It is so important to be clear and to have a pristine agenda - free direction, intending only Highest and Greatest Good for All.

# *Summary of Chapter 1*

## Our Personal Energy Management System

Please reflect upon this section of your personal energy management system. How aligned and centered are you across all platforms of physical, emotional, mental and spiritual/energetic areas?

_____

_____

_____

_____

_____

_____

_____

_____

_____

_____

_____

_____

_____

_____

_____

_____

Are there specific areas or patterns you notice that you wish to change in some way?

_____

_____

_____

_____

_____

_____

_____

_____

_____

_____

_____

_____

_____

_____

_____

_____

_____

_____

_____

What areas are you most comfortable with / grateful for?

_____

_____

_____

_____

_____

_____

_____

_____

_____

_____

_____

_____

_____

*Rejoice in your ability to manifest from energy into matter and enJoy the adventure. Life is afoot!*

# Chapter 2

# Energy

# Anatomy

# Introduction

# Making the Invisible Visible

We are energy. And we have an energetic anatomy profile.

But, how to make the invisible visible?

The visionary artist, Alex Grey, presents us with one vision of physical, energy and spiritual anatomy in *Sacred Mirrors*, his groundbreaking unique set of 21 paintings spanning body, mind and spirit.

His set begins with a silhouette of a human form superimposed on the elemental chart, reminding us of our biochemical foundations. The 2nd painting depicts detailed physical anatomy of our skeletal system. We continue with the complex layering on of nerves, cardiovascular and lymph systems in paintings 3, 4, and 5.

Plate 6 is a comprehensive drawing of our inner viscera and Plate 7 is a meticulous and fascinating image of a human with muscles in place show-casing a pregnant woman with a cutout view of the fetus growing in the womb.

When reflecting on the remarkable pieces of this comprehensive art work one realization is that although we are aware that we are made of bones, circulating blood, muscles and organ systems, when looking at plates 1 – 7 there is a compelling fascination and a dawning sense of shock that this is, indeed, who and what we are. This is our biological origin story. We know this, and yet, it doesn't really look like us at all.

At the 8th -13th set of plates, the envelope of skin is completed and we greet the human being who we think we know. Grey presents male and female representations of Caucasian, African and Asian couples. And, our kaleidoscopic view of human being settles into familiarity.

When we look in the mirror, or when we look at our own or others' bodies, the known internal components are not visible and therefore seem alien to our eyes. Yes, we know we have a skeleton, but that skeleton does not look like the person who looks back at us in the mirror. Yes, we know we have muscles and kidneys and lymph glands, but, again, seeing them on the page seems slightly alien to our sense of self.

Then come plates 14, 15 and 16. And the kaleidoscope vision begins again, but from the opposite perspective.

Plate 14 details energy anatomy. Here we see the systems that transduce energy down into physical, instead of building upward from elemental. It is a fascinating view, and one that energy workers use as their template for healing, balance and empowerment. Grey names this the 'Psychic Energy System'.

The 15th plate brings Alex Grey's visionary art up to a level only clairvoyants might see, what he terms, the 'Spiritual Energy System'. This view of human is more humanoid in appearance, with lines of life force emanating as a vivid toroid around the beginning chakra system and human shaping.

The 'Universal Light Matrix' is Grey's 16th plate in the series. This plate is an unbounded visionary depiction of us, in pure energy form.

It's hard to recognize oneself in the Universal Light Matrix, or even the Spiritual Energy System. But, then, it is just hard to recognize oneself from the earliest plates. We see ourselves in 3D in plates 8-13, the envelope of our skin. But that doesn't mean that the muscle, bone and viscera systems are not in place. We know they are there and they are working to keep us in human form.

So, too, do energy workers know that energy anatomy is in place and that our energetic systems also work to keep us in human form. We know and work from the perspective of energy transducing downwards into physical rather than the well documented elemental evolving upwards every school child knows.

# Chapter 2 Overview

Chapter 2, Energy Anatomy, allows us to reflect upon this anatomical layering so that we may become more familiar and comfortable with this perspective of being human.

The True Mirror, Section 5, allows us to start our journey from energy ('cannot be created or destroyed'). We begin with Spirit Incarnate.

We move next into our actual energy anatomy in Section 6, including auras, energy fields, subtle bodies, and chakras. Angelic musculature and Lightbody Merkaba fields are also discussed.

Intuition, 'the clairs' or higher gift orders are covered in Section 7 as are boundaries, protections and understandings of earthly incarnations. Section 8 concludes with numerous ways to keep in contact with our Spirit selves.

EnJoy the journey within!

# Section 5

## The True Mirror

Visualize that you are in a beautiful crystalline room, filled with iridescent colors and soft harmonic tones. The walls seem to pulse with a warm heartbeat. Right ahead of you is a large oval mirror in a beautiful frame. The frame has words scrolled across the top of the oval and you step closer to read the words.

### *"The True Mirror"*

You look at the image in surprise. What could it mean? Because it doesn't really seem like a mirror. At least not any mirror that you know, because you can't see your face or clothing or any image that looks familiar to you. You might think it's a beautiful painting, because you are drawn to the image and to the colors and feelings invoked in you.

But it's not a painting, because you are shocked to realize that it is moving!

What can it be?

Something is familiar about the image. Then it hits you, 'viscerally', or, more accurately, 'intuitively'. This IS a true mirror. It is the mirror vision of you, in your energetic anatomical form. The 'you' that is eternal, the 'you' that is truly 'you'.

1. Have you looked in the True Mirror?  Close your mind's eye for a moment and look in the Mirror.  Then draw, sketch or write what you see. How does it feel to have a Lightbody?

---

_____

_____

_____

_____

_____

_____

_____

_____

_____

_____

_____

_____

_____

_____

_____

Many young children, especially if they had religious training, were taught that you have a soul. But, do we 'have' a soul?

There is another way to consider the discarnate part of us.

Consider a model of reality in which we are Spirit, eternal, powerful, magnificent. And we incarnate part of who we are for this grand adventure and this moment in physicality and in time. The larger part of us resides in non-physical. And we send out extensions of ourselves for the joy of it.

Scientists tell us that energy cannot be created or destroyed. How, then, does energy and pure consciousness incarnate into the physical 3D reality we call Earth?

Energy Anatomy gives us structures. Energy Systems gives us drivers.

And, here we are!

# Section 6

## Energy Anatomy Structures

Just as our physical body has anatomical structures and functions, our energy body does as well. In this chapter we touch upon the aura, chakras, subtle bodies, channels and meridians. There is space provided for research, feedback, personal understandings, and reflections on practicing these energetic structures.

These next two chapters contain information gotten from esoteric, spiritual, psychic, gnostic or inner knowings and from ancient knowledge that has been passed down to us. These current times are not 'burning times' and, therefore, this information is more readily available. Although you may have to suffer through being called 'woo woo', weird, kooky, and the like from those who don't know about these topics and are afraid to venture into this wonderful realm.

Much of the information in the following 2 sections, energy anatomy and energy systems, have come to us by those using higher sense orders – clairvoyance (clear seeing), clairaudience (clear hearing), clairsentience (clear sensing) and claircognizance (clear knowing). In the future there will come a day when these rarified structures can be viewed by all people with subtle instruments or vibratory/quantum technology. At that time we might need new job descriptions and college certifications to do energy work.

## Different perceptions and models of reality

As we are all working now on ancient writings and inner visions, people might 'view' anatomy or structures from disparate angles. They might see different colors in the aura or in the chakras and interpret the colors differently. This can still be in integrity as we perceive and then filter vibrations through our own sense channels, unique cognitive processes, personal and specialized vocabulary, and individualized experience. Those all allow for differences in perception and interpretation.

There are volumes written and channeled by many wonderful authors on each of these topics and more. This manual presents only a brief overview because we make use of some of energy anatomy structures in our energy healing work, although we necessarily don't have to. Working with energy anatomy and energy systems is a particular model of reality.

Healings are integrated all the time without the knowledge of chakras or subtle bodies. People heal with allopathic medicines, even extremely toxic ones. People heal with prayers, placebos, time, even laughter. As energy healing Lightworkers, many of us choose this particular energetic model. It is our joy to work in what we perceive to be the energy anatomy fields.

Follow your guidance and your interest in learning and working with energy anatomy. It's an interesting challenge to walk a nuanced path between knowledge/experience of energy anatomy and the immediate joy of hands-on healing without any filters, models or an extensive knowledge base. We are always learning and growing. The universe is a big place!

Sometimes people are so enamored of chakras, auras, seeing colors, reading fields, making predictions, etc. that they get distracted and sidelined from the original joys of healing and Lightwork. In my personal model of reality, these energy fields and structures exist, but I keep a light focus and interest. I am not over-enamored or feel I need to read and study more and more. My purpose and passion is to be a Lightworker. My understandings come from within.

It was the same for me as a psychology and counseling student. Theories of personality held light interest for me (especially as I considered them missing crucial elements). My purpose and passion was to hold a hand of hope out to clients and to shine light in their dark shadows.

There is a purity and clarity of intent that we can continually reach for. Be clear of who you are and what work you want to do. Then, ask for help and step forward!

1. What is it that you wish, in your heart of hearts, to do as a Lightworker?

_____

_____

_____

_____

_____

2. What is your knowledge of chakras, auras, and energy fields? Where have you gotten this knowledge? How have you worked with them?

_____

_____

_____

_____

_____

_____

_____

3.  Do you believe energy anatomy structures are real? How do you know?

_____

_____

_____

_____

_____

_____

_____

4.  Reflect back upon your early childhood.

Do you remember a time when you 'knew' something that seemed outside the approved societal view of what is possible to be known? Have you ever seen colors around a person?

_____

_____

_____

_____

_____

_____

_____

_____

5. Were you told you were 'only' imagining something you thought was real?

_____

_____

_____

_____

_____

_____

_____

6. Did you ever feel strongly that someone was saying one thing to you and you knew that was not true?

_____

_____

_____

_____

_____

_____

_____

_____

7.  Were you ever shamed or taught to be frightened for seeing or hearing things others didn't?

_____

_____

_____

_____

_____

_____

_____

_____

_____

8.  Were you encouraged in your personal, unique perspectives?

_____

_____

_____

_____

_____

_____

_____

9. Visualize what it would be like in a society that understands this basic energy anatomy of auras or electromagnetic fields which carry and broadcast our personal coded 'information'.

_____

_____

_____

_____

_____

_____

_____

_____

_____

_____

_____

# The Human Energy Field, the 'Aura'

Although mystical sounding, auras are energy fields around a body. Our bodies have electromagnetic fields surrounding us, sometimes called the human energy field, or aura. This field is often described as oval shaped, as if we exist and move within an egg shaped bubble of energy exquisitely and sensitively permeable to All There Is, to Spirit, to Earth, to our life journeys and companions.

This energy field vibrates, or broadcasts, our personal unique frequency, our 'energetic signature'. Our thoughts, dreams, visions, understandings, emotions, life experiences, and legacies are projected through our fields.

We all read each other's fields much more than we realize. In fact, we are trained at an early age to ignore or deny our knowingness. In part, this is in integrity as we all have inviolate right to our privacy from others. It is impolite, at best, to push ourselves into 'reading' another person without their permission. (I call this 'psychic snooping'.)

However, being trained to ignore this inner knowing, we deny and lessen our innate gifts. Perhaps we might feel confused as children as we 'know' on a visceral or gut level one thing and yet are told the opposite. Perhaps we were ridiculed or frightened when we communicated our truth. We collude with a 'reality' that we are separate from the whole. We are trained to think we exist alone and that our sense of self begins and ends with the envelope of our skin. Science is beginning to prove this as false. Those who are sensitives or intuitives already know this.

Aside from being trained away from reading others or from sensing unseen or misperceived environments (fairies?), we also are encouraged not to perceive what is in our own field. Instead our time is structured for us so that we focus on pre-chosen external details (school subjects and rules, life chores and details, technology, distractions, and more).

Thus, the modern human of today is taught to live their lives in a sea of connection and wonder, yet feel isolated and alone. Kabir once said, "It makes me laugh when I hear that the fish in the water is thirsty." We really are trained to be that thirsty fish!

## Electro-magnetic fields

We all have seen a picture of the Earth's magnetic field, a beautiful, unique spiral shape which is generated from the Earth's core. This electromagnetic field shields our planet from the solar wind particles that could seriously damage life if not deflected by our geomagnetic field. The Earth's field, interacting with the solar particles gifts us the Aurora Borealis and the Aurora Australis, the crowning and natural light displays around the north and south poles. They could be poetically called our Earth's aura.

The latest images from NASA's Voyager 1 and 2 probes have sent back data confirming that our Sun's electromagnetic field extends millions of miles further than was thought possible. The magnetic lines cross in bubble patterns 100 million miles wide at the conjunction where our final solar influence meets interstellar space, thus forming a magnetic bubble shield around our entire solar system. The electromagnetic lines from the sun and the magnetic bubbles could be called our solar aura.

Decades ago, researchers using Kirlian photography, named after Russian engineer, Semyon Kirlian, found electromagnetic fields around plants. Using this electrical photography, plants were found to have a luminous aura around their edges. Even when a tip was cut off, the aura would photograph as whole. Although moisture might be confounding the results, still this is tantalizing information that might be a forerunner of making the invisible visible. Could this be called plant auras?

This type of research and experimentation is still at the frontiers of accepted science. We live in a time when dominant core belief systems do not allow for climate change, much less research into 'taboo' areas.

But, it is not a large leap to make correlations between the electromagnetic fields of the sun, earth, and living plants, to electromagnetic auras around humans. It is only a matter of time and appropriate technology that we will all be able to 'see' the auras around people, around organs, around healthy people, and all types of diseases.

The human aura, or energy field, is a natural occurrence and at this time only those with intuitive gifts are able to 'see' them.

## Can anybody see auras?

An interesting hypothesis is that anyone can see auras. Softening the gaze, looking peripherally, and having a person stand against a light, but neutral background all help.

However, as with much of the intuitive arts, there is variation on the color, scope and meaning of auras and well as the desire, motivation, and belief that it is possible to see auras – by you!  Some people are special. Maybe you think you are 'ordinary' and can't see auras? People might see different colors and interpret them differently. Perhaps you went to a workshop where a machine took a picture of your aura or electrical field. And then the machine interpreted the colors for you?

We are vibrational interpreters and we have unique interpretation skills! The quality of interpretation varies tremendously in this nascent field. If you want to see auras, you can. But, 'see' means ?? The next section on intuition and 'the clairs' will give you more information on your more dominant perceptors.

## What is a Halo?

We have all seen medieval and Renaissance pictures of holy people, saints and sages with a halo, or circle of light, around their head. Halos are the part of the human aura that encircles the head, like the Aurora Borealis encircling the crown of the Earth.

10. Have you ever seen a halo on someone?

_____

_____

_____

_____

_____

_____

_____

# Components of the Human Energy System

As a multidimensional attribute, the human energy system (aura) transduces conscious intent to incarnate (soul) into human form. It is interconnected on many levels and dimensions. There are a number of specific structures in the design of making spirit flesh that have been discerned from ancient times until the present.

These are the subtle bodies, the chakra system, energy channels, and meridians.

## Subtle bodies

Looking at the perspective from the physical, the subtle bodies which are enclosed within the aura or human energy field, are comprised of layers of vibrating fields, each level vibrating higher than the previous level. They all interpenetrate to comprise the incarnating human.

So from the perspective of physicality, the layers rise in vibration:

1. Physical body
2. Etheric double
3. Emotional body
4. Mental body
5. Spiritual bodies

From the perspective of incarnating into physicality, the layers lower in vibration to match Earth density:

1. Spirit
2. Mental body
3. Emotional body
4. Etheric double
5. Physical body

## Short Form

Described above, the short form comprises the basic subtle body structure.

The layer right above the physical is known as the 'etheric' level. This is the body double, on the subtle level, which stores information about the physical including shock and trauma.

The next layer up is the emotional body. Connected closely to the physical through hormonal connectors, the emotional body is a repository of our emotional memories, outside of time constraints.

The mental body is the next layer upwards. These are our thoughts, memories and mental processes, again outside of time. Past life and karmic information can reside here. Of course, there are strong interconnections between mental and emotional states and this impacts our conscious and unconscious patterns and attractions.

The spiritual body is the next layer. It links us to the collective consciousness of the planet, to the higher and greater parts of ourselves that is still in non-physical, and to the spiritual dimension. Many esoteric systems designate additional bodies between the mental and spiritual, naming them the lower and higher mental and the causal layers, but I have included them all in this spiritual body layer.

## Long Form

Information on subtle bodies are present throughout history and throughout channeled information. There is agreement on the presence and vibration levels of subtle bodies. There are changes in names and more detailed levels between mental and spiritual levels.

The more extensive listing of the subtle bodies include:

1. Etheric body: body information

2. Emotional body

3. Mental body

4. Astral, Psychic, Causal, or Higher Mental body: various names are given this space which is seen as a bridge to astral realm and spirit

5. Etheric template: blueprint

6. Spiritual, Soul, Celestial, or Diamond body

7. Integrated, Causal, or Ketheric: various names for template for your soul

Regardless of names and specificity, these interrelating energy fields store vast amounts of information about our present life, our motivations, challenges, dis-eases, and soul contracts. It also stores information about the soul's incarnations.

*Spectrum Energetics* and *SoulAnge Harmonics* are two advanced energy healing systems taught in the Lightworker Orientation and Training Apprenticeship at Arise. Both systems work extensively with the subtle bodies and with the chakra systems. This work calls for a high level of integrity in accessing and interpreting the coded information held within our subtle bodies.

Next up, the chakra system.

# The Major Chakras

Chakra is a Sanskrit word for 'wheel'. Those who 'see' these esoteric energy centers describe them as moving wheels, transposing energy from an unbound state into energy that is used by our bodies to keep us alive and well. Simply put, chakras funnel energy from our subtle energy fields into our organs and physical structures so we can incarnate and have fun on planet Earth.

There are 7 major chakras in the body, with increasing attention being given to a chakra above the head and one below the body.

Chakras are an interesting part of our energy anatomy and it is good to spend some time understanding them. Each chakra corresponds to physical body areas and organs. They are traditionally paired with colors and have much information to teach us.

The best way to research chakras is to spend time with each one on yourself. Give yourself Reiki on each chakra. Be present and ask for information to come to you. We are vibrational interpreters and information is flowing around us at all times. We need to tune into the frequency we desire, just like tuning a radio station. It is as easy to understand as we understand the dynamics behind radio transmission.

As you research and spend time with your own chakras, add to the information on each chakra. Draw them, become familiar with them, and enjoy this magnificent and elegant energy organ system.

## 1<sup>st</sup> Chakra

The first chakra is found at the base of your torso. It is often associated with the color red. If you are visualizing the color, consider lightening the red so that it is vibrant and vital.

This chakra is associated with safety, security, groundedness, ease of being in physical form. It is also related to the sex organs and reproductive system, overall health, the lower half of the body, and to trust and faith issues.

11. Reflect and research the 1<sup>st</sup> chakra.

_____

_____

_____

_____

_____

_____

_____

_____

_____

_____

_____

_____

_____

_____

12. Put your hands on your 1<sup>st</sup> chakra and give yourself Reiki. What do you notice? How does your chakra look or feel? Do you notice any impressions or messages that come to you from your 1st chakra?

_____

_____

_____

_____

_____

_____

_____

_____

_____

_____

_____

_____

_____

_____

_____

_____

## 2nd Chakra

The 2nd chakra is located an inch below your navel. The 2nd chakra is often associated with the color orange, consider visualizing it as a bright joyful orange.

It is connected to your adrenal gland, immune system, sexual and reproductive organs and functions. It is connected to love relationships, marriage, pregnancy, labor, childbirth, child rearing, and Inner Child.

13. Reflect and research the 2nd chakra.

_____

_____

_____

_____

_____

_____

_____

_____

_____

_____

_____

_____

_____

_____

14. Put your hands on your 2nd chakra and give yourself Reiki. What do you notice? How does your chakra look or feel? Do you notice any impressions or messages that come to you from your 2nd chakra?

_____

_____

_____

_____

_____

_____

_____

_____

_____

_____

_____

_____

_____

_____

## 3rd Chakra

The 3rd chakra is located at your solar plexus point. This chakra is traditionally associated with the color yellow. It is associated with the pancreas and metabolism.

The attributes of this chakra are power, control and identity. Who or what has power or control over you? How do you identify yourself?

This is an important chakra for our culture and time period since most of us have been raised since our earliest years to be in obedience to others' power and control. Many people feel blocked energies in this chakra. Some people feel pain when getting Reiki in this area.

If this is the case for you, then consider giving extra Reiki to yourself on your 3rd chakra every day. You might also consider asking for information and help to release the constraints in this area.

15. Reflect and research the 3rd chakra.

_____

_____

_____

_____

_____

_____

_____

_____

_____

_____

_____

_____

16. Put your hands on your 3rd chakra and give yourself Reiki. What do you notice? How does your chakra look or feel? Do you notice any impressions or messages that come to you from your 3rd chakra?

_____

_____

_____

_____

_____

_____

_____

_____

_____

_____

_____

_____

_____

_____

_____

_____

_____

## 4th Chakra

The 4th chakra is located at the heart center. It is often associated with the colors green and, more recently, pink. The 4th chakra brings energy to our heart, lungs, and entire circulatory and respiratory systems as well as the thymus gland and the immune system.

Associated with love and marriage, the heart chakra also emanates unconditional love, compassion, mercy and higher loving relations.

17. Reflect and research the 4th chakra.

_____

_____

_____

_____

_____

_____

_____

_____

_____

_____

_____

_____

_____

_____

18. Put your hands on your 4th chakra and give yourself Reiki. What do you notice? How does your chakra look or feel? Do you notice any impressions or messages that come to you from your 4th chakra?

_____

_____

_____

_____

_____

_____

_____

_____

_____

_____

_____

_____

_____

_____

_____

_____

_____

## 5th Chakra

The 5th chakra is located at the base of the throat. It is commonly associated with the color blue.

The throat chakra is aligned with communications of all kinds, verbal and non-verbal, as well as the thyroid gland. What message are you broadcasting? How well do you reach outwards? The throat chakra is also associated with speaking your truth and living your truth.

19. Reflect and research the 5th chakra.

_____

_____

_____

_____

_____

_____

_____

_____

_____

_____

_____

_____

_____

20. Put your hands on your 5th chakra and give yourself Reiki. What do you notice? How does your chakra look or feel? Do you notice any impressions or messages that come to you from your 5th chakra?

_____

_____

_____

_____

_____

_____

_____

_____

_____

_____

_____

_____

_____

_____

_____

_____

_____

## 6<sup>th</sup> Chakra

The 6<sup>th</sup> chakra is located in the middle of your brow and is often called the 3<sup>rd</sup> eye chakra. It is traditionally associated with the color indigo, or dark blue.

The 6<sup>th</sup> chakra brings energy to our mental and brain functions including the pituitary, hypothalamus, and often pineal gland as well.

21. Reflect and research the 6<sup>th</sup> chakra.

_____

_____

_____

_____

_____

_____

_____

_____

_____

_____

_____

_____

_____

_____

_____

_____

22. Put your hands on your 6th chakra and give yourself Reiki. What do you notice? How does your chakra look or feel? Do you notice any impressions or messages that come to you from your 6th chakra?

_____

_____

_____

_____

_____

_____

_____

_____

_____

_____

_____

_____

_____

_____

_____

_____

## 7<sup>th</sup> Chakra

The 7<sup>th</sup> chakra lies at the top of your head, and is known as the crown chakra. Usually associated with the color purple, the crown chakra opens in a cone shape with the larger end pointing upwards. The crown chakra reflects our openness to Source Energy.

23. Reflect and research the 7<sup>th</sup> chakra.

_____

_____

_____

_____

_____

_____

_____

_____

_____

_____

_____

_____

_____

_____

_____

_____

24. Put your hands on your 7th chakra and give yourself Reiki. What do you notice? How does your chakra look or feel? Do you notice any impressions or messages that come to you from your 7th chakra?

_____

_____

_____

_____

_____

_____

_____

_____

_____

_____

_____

_____

_____

_____

_____

_____

## Earth Chakra

Although not traditionally associated with the 7 major chakras, the Earth Chakra, located below the feet, about a foot into the earth, is gaining more attention. The Earth chakra connects us with Gaia energies and the partnership we share incarnating on Earth.

25. Reflect and research the Earth chakra.

_____

_____

_____

_____

_____

_____

_____

_____

_____

_____

_____

_____

_____

_____

_____

_____

26. Direct your hands downward, intending your gaze onto a cone shape below your feet and into the Earth, at your Earth Chakra and give Reiki to yourself and to the Gaia partnership. What do you notice? How does your chakra look or feel? Do you notice any impressions or messages that come to you from your Earth chakra?

_____

_____

_____

_____

_____

_____

_____

_____

_____

_____

_____

_____

_____

_____

_____

_____

## Soul Star Chakra

Although not traditionally associated with the 7 major chakras, the Soul Star Chakra, located about a foot above your head, is gaining more attention. The Soul Star Chakra connects us with Divine Love, spiritual energies, and known as the seat of the soul. This chakra also connects us to solar and galactic energies, and the higher partnerships with share.

27. Reflect and research the soul star chakra.

_____

_____

_____

_____

_____

_____

_____

_____

_____

_____

_____

_____

_____

_____

_____

28. Direct your attention above your head and turn your palms upward toward a cone shape about a foot above your head, and give yourself Reiki at your Soul Star Chakra. What do you notice? How does your chakra look or feel? Do you notice any impressions or messages that come to you from your Soul Star chakra?

_____

_____

_____

_____

_____

_____

_____

_____

_____

_____

_____

_____

_____

_____

_____

_____

_____

## Chakra Meditation

Every day, consider bathing your chakras in a loving embrace. You can start in the order we have studied them, 1st, 2nd, 3rd, 4th, 5th, 6th, 7th, Earth, and circle back to the Soul Star.

_____

_____

_____

_____

_____

_____

_____

_____

_____

_____

_____

_____

_____

_____

_____

_____

## Clear, Align, and Balance Chakras

Chakras, being multidimensional organs, have a multitude of purposes. Transposing energy into our physical vehicle is one important facet. They also hold memories, trauma, stories, empowering information, and are homes for our Inner Child and Inner Wise One.

With Reiki training, you are taught to clear, align, and balance your chakras daily. With *Spectrum Energetics* training, you will work exclusively with the chakra system, getting detailed information and setting healings in the chakras for physical, mental, emotional and spiritual issues.

For those with Reiki 1 and 2 training, the easiest way to clear your chakras is to put Cho Ku Rei, the power symbol, on your body as a whole and then draw the power symbol over each chakra every day.  This simple practice, which can be done in a few seconds, will help to bring your energy field into integrity especially if it is shredded through trauma and the wounded healer pathway. It will also clear and align your chakras.

You can energize your chakras by visualizing or wearing colors associated with that chakra. Each of the traditional colors associated with the chakras follow a rainbow model. Some people interpret different colors with various chakras. Again, we are vibrational interpreters and color is a vibrational frequency. If you see a different color, visualize that color and discern what it means for you.

29. Spend 2-3 minutes each day for a week consciously cleaning, aligning and balancing your chakras. Do you notice a difference?

_____

_____

_____

_____

_____

30. Stop your practice for a day or two. Do you notice a difference?

_____

_____

_____

_____

_____

## Energy Channels and Meridians

Finally, there are energy channels and meridians running throughout our entire body. They look like energy roadways with little points dotted throughout our body.  Most people who are aware of acupuncture, acupressure, and Shiatsu are familiar with the placement and even feelings associated with various energy points on their body.

These pathways carry energy to every organ in the body. Based upon Chinese medicine, there are over 400 acupuncture points and 12 meridians including central, governing, spleen, heart, small intestine, bladder, kidney, circulation, triple warmer, gall bladder, liver, lung, large intestine, and stomach.

If you are interested in these areas, consider studying Chinese medicine. Most energy healers do not delve as deeply into the meridian and channel system, focusing more upon the chakra and subtle bodies. However, we are guided with information directed through our personal interests, constructs and vocabulary. If you are familiar with these Chinese healing paradigms, then you can get information for your client through this extensive system.

# Increasing Awareness of Your Energy Field

As we work our way through the Apprenticeship, begin to notice the 'messages', 'signs', or 'information' that pops out at you. Quantum physics describes our existing in a 'unified, entangled field'. We call the field surrounding us, the human energy field, the aura, the chakra system.

Consciously working with our field we increase our intuitive gifts. Practice. Notice when you get feedback or information. Check the information. If it has verifiable information, don't say, "That's weird." Or, "I don't know why/how/what..." By minimizing the information, we minimize the flow of information. By denying our truth and our intuitive perception, we lessen the volume of the messaging.

On the opposite spectrum, sometimes people wait for or interpret everything as a 'sign'. They won't take an action or make a decision unless there are 'signs'. Sometimes, the signals are diffuse, and hard to read.

Information is like a moving river. We track the river of life, the river of truth, the river of interconnectedness. Sometimes it is swelling and unmistakable, other times it's a trickle. Harder still when you need a dousing rod to find water. Or, you might need to dig. It's all part of this wonderful game we call life on planet Earth. EnJoy the game!

## Physical body and medical intuitives

It is very possible to access information from your conscious unified field concerning your physical body. Learn to scan your body, ask questions of your body. What does it need? What is really going on behind a symptom or illness? What can you do to make your body more comfortable and radiantly healthy?

These are all good questions to ask yourself. Kryon and Lee Carroll speak about Innate Intelligence. Research their understandings about the bridge we are building (again) to our innate wisdom.

Do a body scan. Talk to an organ. Spend time visiting a sickness. Bring chicken soup, and listen.

Take responsibility for your physical vehicle, in sickness and in health, loving and honoring yourself moment by moment, breath by breath, situation by situation, day in and day out.

## Mental and emotional detectives

Mentally and emotionally, we believe thoughts and emotions come and go with no rhyme or reason. It was life altering for me when I learned that our feelings come from thoughts, and that we can have control of our thoughts, and therefore, our feelings.

It is our responsibility as Lightworkers to shine our light clearly. If our light is filtered through layers of family/social/peer/media filters then we are probably shining muddied light and clarity. Go within, clear up your inner landscape.

Work with the law of attraction, pursue personal guided work to understand the engines (and, yes, sometimes demons) that can drive you. Take responsibility for your vibrational set point so you know what you are vibrating out into the world.

Like a detective, follow the thread of your hurt, pain, anguish, grief, guilt, fear... any and all emotions. Track the river of truth to the source. Release, feel the relief. Clear the emotions as best you can. Be grateful that you are understanding the thread of it all. Be compassionate and loving with yourself. Be accepting and creative with the source of the discomfort, whether a person or a situation. Design some loving, light-filled, and smiling affirmations.

And, when similar thoughts arise again (and they will), begin to realize you have a choice in the matter of whether you want to play with that thought again or not. Perhaps, after a few times, you can put the thought memory aside with the Sei He Ki, mental and emotional healing Reiki symbol. Or, send to the situation (past, present or future) with Hon Sha Ze Sho Nen.

Take responsibility for your mental and emotional landscape, moment by moment, breath by breath, situation by situation, day in and day out.

## Spiritual warriors and sages

As you begin to access higher dimensions of your energy field, be prepared for the power of your dignity, clarity, devotion and dedication to become more apparent to you. We have lived lifetime after lifetime (if that is your model of reality), we are Old Souls, and we have walked a spiritual path for many of them. We have suffered and probably died for much of our wisdom. And this soul wisdom does not abandon us as we incarnate. It is in our field. And we are learning to access that wisdom we have dearly paid for.

Meditate. Read inspirational texts and poems. Connect with nature.

Take responsibility for your connection within, with Spirit, with Divinity, and with Your Divinity, moment by moment, breath by breath, situation by situation, day in and day out.

# Section 7

## Intuition and 'The Clairs'

## Intuition

We tune in and decode the information embedded in the energy around us. We all can do this! Practice, believe in yourself, and know that this process is natural. Ask for help in opening more fully to your gifts.

You may have had a "weird" experience, or two, or more. "Weird" because it was outside what we normally call 'normal'. But, if we are physical vehicles of Spirit/energy incarnating through energy organs and systems (previous section), then it is 'normal' to have heightened senses because we are in fact energy fields interconnected with other energy fields. And, as our scientists tell us, time is not linear and therefore we can access people and information from the past as well as the present, and even the future. This is all normal!

For the purpose of this Apprenticeship, we walk a middle path. We honor and practice intuitive gifts. But, as Lightworkers, we don't get distracted. We are here to feel good and to shine our light. Intuition helps us feel good and helps us shine our light where and when it is needed.

## Imagination vs. Intuition

We have all had experiences of using our imagination, where we enjoy making up a story or a game. Using our imagination is creative play and makes our lives sparkle; sometimes imagination can even help us survive. As children we use our imagination often and freely, and are socially trained that our imagination is also known as 'lies'. Imagination is also known as kid stuff, not real, not for adults. "Just imagination" implies "less than".

So, we often find ourselves in a quandary when we first intend to open to our intuitive skills as a healer and Lightworker. Are we making up the image or the message that seems to come to us 'out of the blue'?

Consider that we are pioneers striking out on new territory. Our intent is pure; we do not wish to deceive people. Our egos are in check; we do not wish to have people think we are psychic wonders.

We are intending to open to a larger broadcast than we frequently tune into. Within this intent for a larger wavelength, we are intending for specific information for a client or a situation to use for healing, balance, and empowerment. This is our ability and our responsibility to open ourselves, in integrity, and to access higher information and guidance for ourselves and others. This is normal communication, although not normal or common in our present society. Indigenous peoples around the world have accessed this greater pool of communication for thousands of years. We can, too.

Be compassionate with yourself and be patient! It might take a little coaxing for you to relax, trust that this can be real, receive messages, correctly learn to interpret the messages, and correctly learn to communicate them.

As young students, as we are trained out of our imaginations, we are trained into 'critical thinking skills', logical, if/then scenarios. So, we work our way backwards to finding, appreciating, and encouraging our imaginations again. And then work with your imagination symbols so that you can easily discern the 'feel' or the 'vibration' of your imagination. It has a vibratory signature. It feels good, and fun, and creative, and expansive.

By allowing yourself the permission to use your imagination again, you will become very familiar with your creativity. But, intuition goes beyond this area. Intuition is an area right above imagination and there can be grey areas involved. Are we imagining seeing a bear during a session or is the bear an intuitive symbol, meaning something more? You are the one to discern the difference because you are the one receiving the symbol or message and learning to correctly interpret it.

There is a fine line between imagination and intuition, and there is another fine line, in the beginning, between intuition and guided information. Each feels distinctly different. Intuition, and especially guided information, feels lighter, more loving, more expansive, and more whole. You can ask where this information is coming from and wait to hear an answer, or a name.

# Higher Gift Orders, or 'The Clairs'

We interpret this physical existence through our senses. And each of our senses range on a vibrational scale. As we ascend higher on the non-physical side, our senses heighten to bring in more information. This is a normal, although not well understood or well taught process.

It is part of Spirit incarnating in a physical human vehicle that we see, hear, smell, taste, touch, feel, think and interpret vibrations of all kinds. Bats and dolphins use sonar. It is not 'unnatural'. It is one of their primary vibrational interpreters. Beethoven was deaf towards the end of his life and still he composed exquisitely beautiful music. He cut the legs off his piano, laid on the floor, and 'felt' the music vibrationally. His process was not 'unnatural' – more like 'supernatural' but still vibrationally interpretive.

Our normal senses and interpreters can be elevated and tune into higher frequencies in which we are all connected, through time, space and dimension. This is, as physicists call it, an entangled field. We are entangled with each other. Neither time, space, nor dimension are barriers. This concept is a difficult one to understand, unless you are well versed in science fiction literacy and time travel enigmas. Regardless of our literary treats, we can all learn to heighten our gifts and step through time and space!

Clair'     in French means 'clear'. The most well-known higher gift orders are:

- Clairvoyance - clear seeing

- Clairaudience – clear hearing

- Clairsentience – clear feeling

- Claircognizance – clear knowing

The lesser known ones are:

- Clairtangence - clear touching or psychometry

- Clairgustance - clear tasting

- Clairscent - clear smelling, also known as clairalience

Let's get to know more of each kind:

## Clairvoyance

Clear seeing, mental images, seeing visions, seeing those who are not in physical form… there are so many ways to experience clear sight. It seems that of all the 'clairs', clairvoyance is the most referenced and the most glamorous. It is hard to ignore someone who says, "Your mother is standing right next to you. She is wearing a maroon coat with a broach that looks like a ladybug." If your mom always wore a maroon coat and such a pin, it is hard not to believe everything else the person might say to you.

Clairvoyants can sometimes see lights flickering or sparking, especially out of the corner of eyes. They usually have a great sense of visual beauty or harmony. With clairvoyance, you might see a certain configuration of numbers repeatedly (like 444), or often see feathers, hummingbirds or dragon flies. Ask who is visiting.

Most Lightworkers are not highly clairvoyant, at least at the start of their practice. Many times I have heard students judge themselves harshly that they "can't see anything". And, therefore, they judge themselves 'not good enough' to do this work. And they can't be more wrong!

When I am able to 'see' during a healing, it appears to me as a soft mental silhouette or daydream, often with a feeling or message attached. It is very rare to have inner sight that is as clear and as defined as 3D viewing.

Close your eyes. It is not pitch black. There are areas of grey, light and dark. There are bands and sometimes swirls. Sometimes the ambient light (from a lamp or the sun) moves into our inner screen. Sometimes you can start telling a story and 'see' the images. Remember and run a scene from a favorite movie. Play with inner story-telling.

To practice more clairvoyance, relaxation is a must. Then belief that it is a sense that can be heightened in you – that you can do this work! Soften the eyes when you are looking for auras or colors in the client's field. Look peripherally not straight on. Or, close your eyes and feel your way in the dark until silhouettes start moving. Stay with the image or scene. Ask internally what are you seeing. Ask what it means for the client.

1. Are you excited about the prospect of being more clairvoyant?

_____

_____

_____

_____

_____

2. Do you believe you can do this?

_____

_____

_____

_____

_____

3. What fears do you have about being clairvoyant?

_____

_____

_____

_____

_____

_____

4. Practice alone, in meditation or in bed. Call upon those you wish to talk to. Contact your Inner Child. Call upon an Angel. Jot down the images. Practice interpreting the images.

_____

_____

_____

_____

_____

_____

_____

_____

_____

_____

_____

_____

_____

_____

5. Practice with a client. When you are in a session, close your eyes and ask for a symbol or a message for that person. Relax, listen to music, follow your inner screen. When a symbol appears from the mist, stay with it. Ask what it means. Don't just assign a meaning or a non-meaning: "I see a bicycle, so go outdoors more and exercise" or, " I see a bike. I have no idea what it means."

   Jot down a few images that have come during a session:

   _____

   _____

   _____

   _____

   _____

   _____

   _____

   _____

   _____

   _____

   _____

   _____

   _____

   _____

# Clairaudience

Clairaudience is heightened hearing, including melodies, songs, and sensitivity to noise in general. You may hear loving, guided information, most times with a vocabulary and cadence that is not your own. Of course, you know the vocabulary, but you don't usually speak, even to yourself, in such a manner.

Once I 'heard' the Sermon on the Mount' being recited as I was waking up. Other times I have heard people talking about me, and it was guided information, not just chitchat.

With clients, if you practice asking, listening, believing you can do it, and dialoguing, you will often 'hear' and speak with Angels, Guides and the client's soul, especially in the advanced healing work of *Living Fractals of Light*, *Spectrum Energetics*, and *SoulAnge Harmonics*.

Most Lightworkers do receive messages, but it is hard to determine whether they are clairaudient, clairsentient, or claircognizant. Again, not being judgmental or impatient helps. Recognizing and honoring when something 'pops in' helps, rather than minimizing and marginalizing messages. And, practice always helps.

As with clairvoyance, during a healing I don't hear voices as normally as we do in 3D (with the exception of those two 'dreams'). You are receiving a 'package' which drops down and there is a sense of someone speaking, telepathically, to you. That seems to be the normal way of receiving clairaudient information, unless this is a major gift and service for you. Otherwise, as a Lightworker, it is a soft, inner sense of dialoguing.

Sometimes, I 'hear' a message as soon as I start the session. Other times I ask for information or start talking to Guides. Verbally posing a question helps. Then wait for the answer. With Angels and devic beings (fairies) in particular, they love giving messages with smiles or laughter associated, such as a play on words or a message with a twist. It's always fun when you can laugh during a session.

To practice more clairaudience, relaxation and believe in yourself is a must. I sometimes sing or hum to begin using my vocal cords. Speaking your way through the session helps start the movement. You could describe their field, or how well they are grounded, then with an interesting area, ask what it is you are seeing or sensing. It does take courage to speak verbally, but it really helps! And, clients are in a light trance state and will rarely question you, unless you have given them information before. Then, be prepared, they will want it again!

6. Are you excited about the prospect of being more clairaudient?

_____

_____

_____

_____

_____

7.  Do you believe you can do this?

_____

_____

_____

_____

_____

_____

_____

8.  What fears do you have about being clairaudient?

_____

_____

_____

_____

_____

_____

_____

_____

9. Practice alone, in meditation or in bed. Call upon those you wish to talk to. Contact your Inner Child. Call upon an Angel. Jot down the messages you receive. Practice interpreting the messages.

_____

_____

_____

_____

_____

_____

_____

_____

_____

_____

_____

_____

_____

_____

_____

_____

_____

_____

_____

10. Practice with a client. When you are in a session, close your eyes and ask for a symbol or a message for that person. Relax, listen to music, open yourself to dialoguing with their Soul, their Guardian Angel, or a Loved One of the Light.  Or, call upon those Guides and Beings you love to work with. Call upon Jesus, Mary, Buddha, Quan Yin, Angels or Archangels. Talk to them and wait for their answer.

Jot down a few messages that have come during a session:

_____

_____

_____

_____

_____

_____

_____

_____

_____

_____

_____

_____

_____

# Clairsentience

Clear sensing, feeling, empathy, and being a 'sensitive' all fall within the clairsentience category. We are speaking of multidimensional sense interpretations, so there is a tendency for guided information to merge when being interpreted (see, feel, hear or 'just know' something) rather than being discrete or linear.

Those who have clairsentience as their primary gift order, are highly compassionate and like to help people or animals. You trust your gut feelings as they are usually accurate.

Clairsentience is the primary heightened sense of most Lightworkers. Most are very much aware of their feelings and of the feelings of people and animals around them. In fact, for most Lightworkers, the opposite is more the problem: how Not to feel so much from others.

Many Lightworkers have come from a 'wounded healer' past where you have had a hard time in childhood or adulthood, in relationships, careers, health or abundance. You have had to work your way through much sorrow, confusion, or even betrayal and abandonment to get here, standing as a Lightworker, beaming hope, optimism, compassion, and spiritual determination.

There is usually an issue of 'torn' or 'shredded' boundaries with Lightworkers who have come from a wounded healer past. Think of a cat's claws on a sheer curtain, with light vertical lines ripped into the fabric. You might be overly sensitive to movies, books, news, people's stories, or people's pain.

You might have anaesthetized yourself in the past to help with your oversensitivity. This can include over drinking, over medicating, over eating, losing oneself in relationships or running from helping one person to another. If you feel overly sensitive to people or situations, especially in our society of high stress and toxicity, then survival instincts kick in to help buffer the poundings. To understand this is to have compassion for yourself, and determination to boundary in better ways.

11. Are you excited about the prospect of being more clairsentient or, of keeping stronger boundaries because you know you are clairsentient?

_____

_____

_____

_____

_____

_____

_____

_____

12. What fears do you have about being clairsentient?

_____

_____

_____

_____

_____

_____

_____

_____

13. Practice clairsentience with another Apprentice. Choose a time to connect and notice how you feel. Is it you or is it them? Jot down the feelings you get. Practice interpreting the meaning.

_____

_____

_____

_____

_____

_____

_____

_____

_____

_____

_____

_____

_____

_____

_____

_____

_____

14. Practice clairsentience with a client. When you are in a session, close your eyes and ask for a symbol or a message for that person. Relax, listen to music, be open to your feelings. Is this coming from you or from them?  How are you able to tell the difference?

Jot down a few feelings that have come during a session:

_____

_____

_____

_____

_____

_____

_____

_____

_____

_____

_____

_____

_____

_____

_____

_____

_____

# Claircognizance

Claircognizance is defined as clear knowing. This higher sense is often associated with clairsentience and there is a lot of overlap with the two. The difference is more of a feeling or empathic nature with clairsentience and knowledge, information, mental clarity, or wisdom 'dropping in' with claircognizance.

With claircognizance, you may be able to know something, including facts, without learning about it before. You may have brilliant ideas, thoughts, inspirations, including ways to make money. You may have premonitions, precognition of future events, déjà vu experiences.

You may enjoy reading and drilling down for deep information, and love sharing that information, especially one-on-one. You may finish another's sentences because you know their thought. And, you might know when someone is lying to you.

15. Are you excited about the prospect of being more claircognizant?

_____

_____

_____

_____

16. Do you believe you can do this?

_____

_____

_____

_____

17. What fears do you have about being claircognizant?

_____

_____

_____

_____

_____

18. Practice sharing information with another Apprentice. Or, ask for information to be 'downloaded' to you about a subject. Sleep on it; write a note and put it under your pillow. Put a textbook next to your pillow and notice if you have more ease in learning or remembering the information.

    Jot down any information or areas you are asking for information. Practice recognizing, accepting, and being grateful for the information that does come. Don't dismiss or minimize your information!

_____

_____

_____

_____

_____

_____

_____

_____

_____

_____

_____

_____

_____

_____

19. Practice with a client. When you are in a session, close your eyes and ask for a symbol or a message for that person concerning an issue they have mentioned, physical, mental, emotional, or spiritual. Relax, listen to music, allow information to arise within you.

Jot down a few images that have come during a session:

_____

_____

_____

_____

_____

_____

_____

_____

_____

_____

_____

_____

_____

_____

_____

# Clairtangence, Clairgustance, Clairscent

Clear touching, tasting and smelling is known as clairtangence, clairgustance, and clairscent, respectively. Clairtangency is feeling intuitively through hands, such as assessing information while scanning a client on the table. Also, with Clairtangence you are able to get information when touching an object that belongs to someone.

Clairgustance, or clear tasting and clairscent, or clear smelling, are interesting higher gifts. You might be able to taste and smell flowers, food, spices, perfumes, incense, coffee, tea, smoke, etc.

I have had an experience of both once in my life and it is exquisite to discern higher vibrations of everyday tastes and scents.

20. Are you excited about the prospect of being more clairtangent, clairgustance or clairscent? Is there one that is more interesting to you than another?

_____

_____

_____

_____

_____

_____

21. Do you believe you can do this?

_____

_____

_____

_____

_____

_____

22. What fears do you have about being clairtangent, clairgustant or clairscent?

_____

_____

_____

_____

_____

_____

_____

23. Practice alone with any of these three 'clairs'.

Jot down what you touched, tasted or smelled. Practice interpreting the sense images.

_____

_____

_____

_____

_____

_____

_____

_____

_____

_____

_____

24. Practice these last three 'clairs' with a client. Although these are more rare, if they do appear (smell roses, vanilla, etc.) Jot them down.

_____

_____

_____

_____

_____

_____

_____

_____

_____

_____

_____

_____

_____

_____

_____

_____

_____

# Summary for Heightening Higher Gifts

Below is a summary outline for heightening your higher gifts. One of 'the clairs' (clairvoyance, clairaudience, clairsentience, claircognizance, clairtangence, clairgustance, and clairscent) is likely your dominant one. For Lightworkers it is often clairsentience. You might then have two additional supplemental gifts or a mélange of a few.

You are an energy being and these are ways of perceiving and interpreting vibrations, something we are expert at, albeit in 3D ranges. Expand and enjoy a larger information access!

1. Identity: Claim your identity as a Lightworker, a sensitive, a healer, etc. What is your main identity? Does this identity allow for more expansive energy perception and interpretation?

2. Ask: Call upon your Guides, your Higher Self, Beings of Love and Light to help you with the higher gift you would love to experience more of.

3. Recognize little messages here and there, a penny here and there, a feather; don't judge,

4. Be grateful for the message; begin to dialogue with the Sender – even your own Higher and wiser self

5. Begin to interpret the message; what could a dragonfly mean at that moment? Were you thinking of someone? Did a name or face pop in?

6. Allow 'packages' to drop in with as little filters as possible

7. Continue dialoguing with Spirit for highest, lightest and most loving interpretation; messages are always positive, loving, and kind

8. Broaden or heighten the message – go higher

9. Learn how to communicate this information without ego, intimidation, false sense of truth or inevitableness

10. Celebrate and stay open, patient, expectant and happy

## A final word about protections and boundaries

As you are working on increasing your intuitive gifts and dialoging with Sprit in new ways, remember to protect yourself, your environment, and keep your field clear and boundaried. It is not necessary to armor yourself or feel fear. We are crossing multiple dimensions when doing this work and we set our conditions and protections.

Protections can be as simple as:

- Surrounding yourself with white light

- Calling upon Archangel Michael, God, Source, Ascended Beings

- Setting a clear intent for the work you wish to do

- Putting Cho Ku Rei on corners of ceiling

- Understanding and reaffirming there is no source of darkness. Darkness is only the absence of light

And, then, enjoy the work you are undertaking, knowing that you are safe and secure and that everything that happens is in the Highest and Greatest Good for All.

As Lightworkers, we understand clearly we are energetic beings living in an energetic universe. People vibrate at various levels and some feel good to us, when we are in close enough resonance.  Usually, we feel very good when someone's vibration is higher than ours. But, it might not feel so good when someone's vibration is much lower or more chaotic than ours.

In a crowded, impersonal situation, it is easier to 'read' these lower vibrations and to leave. You can also put more physical space between yourself and another and this will lessen the impact.

If you are interacting with someone on a more personal level, living with them for example, then you will need to work more diligently to keep your field whole and to handle the dissonance with clarity, compassion and discernment. No one feels good with energy dissonance, so it's not one-sided.

If your work situations calls for you to spend time in a lower energy or more chaotic environment, you have choices and tools.  Putting Reiki symbols on yourself and your work environment is appropriate. What is not appropriate is sending Reiki so someone changes or leaves. Instead, affirm "Highest and Greatest Good" and trust the outcome.

1. Do you set protections and clear boundaries? How do you do this?

_____

_____

_____

_____

_____

_____

_____

_____

_____

Light and love are much more powerful than darkness and fear. Kryon has said, there is almost 2 -1 ratio to balance because light is so powerful. Happiness and well being is our natural state.

"All is well, all is well, all is always well" is a wonderful mantra to help us align with the higher energy field which is really us, in the True Mirror.

Understand this law of the universe!

Live this law and this Joy!

# Section 8

## Keeping in Contact with our Spiritual Selves

As we move forward with our understanding of looking in the True Mirror, of working with human energy field including our subtle bodies and chakra system, and of increasing our intuitive gifts, it is important to keep in contact with our highest and greatest self and with the spiritual dimension.

We do this in a number of ways:

## Meditation

Meditation is going within to your divine state. There are so many methods available today. Even meditating a few minutes a day is good.

1. Do you have a daily meditative practice? What is it?

_____

_____

_____

_____

_____

_____

2. Is there anything else you would like to add right now?

_____

_____

_____

_____

_____

_____

## Prayer

Prayer is connecting and dialoguing with Spirit, God, Creator in a manner that is complementary to meditation but usually seen as more active and engaged.

3.  Do you pray? Do you have a daily time or way you pray?

_____

_____

_____

_____

_____

_____

_____

_____

_____

_____

4.  Is there anything else you would like to add right now?

_____

_____

_____

_____

_____

_____

## Guided Visualization

Visualizations are wonderful ways to open our creative, imaginative, and then intuitive perceptors and feel our way into a higher, multidimensional space. There can be a special portal or doorway to go between dimensions. You can visit safe spaces, future spaces, healing chambers, Hall of Records, Halls of Healing Masters. There are so many wonderful places to go!

5.  Do you work with guided visualizations? How?

_____

_____

_____

_____

_____

6.  Do you have a favorite place or portal to access higher spaces?

_____

_____

_____

_____

_____

7.  Is there anything you would like to add right now?

_____

_____

_____

_____

## Dialogue with spirit: automatic writing

Book 4 of the *Tools for Lightworkers Series, Dialogue with Spirit*, details a step –by- step approach to automatic writing or channeling. It is a wonderful journaling tool in which you partner with Spirit and multidimensional energies and open your telepathic communication skills.

8.  Do you do automatic writing? Do you have a set schedule?

_____

_____

_____

_____

_____

9.  Do you dialogue with one Being in particular or with many?

_____

_____

_____

_____

_____

10. Is there anything you would like to add right now?

_____

_____

_____

_____

_____

## Gratitudes and Affirmations

Books 1 and 2 of the *Tools for Lightworkers Series, Daily DeLights* and *Mandala of Wholeness*, give many examples of affirmations and gratitude journaling. These two well-known practices easily step you into the inner environment in which to receive messages from Spirit. You affirm this is what you want and this is who you are. You are grateful for the opportunity to do this work and capture the small and large incidences of increasing your higher gift orders. Gratitude journaling and affirmations work very well together.

11. Do you regularly work with affirmations and gratitude journaling for increasing your intuitive gifts?

_____

_____

_____

_____

_____

_____

_____

_____

_____

_____

12. Is there anything you would like to add right now?

_____

_____

_____

_____

## Compassion-in-action

Kindness, taking a moment to act like an Angel or Emissary on Earth is a wonderful way to put you in a higher receptive environment for increasing your intuitive gifts. We take our learnings and bring them out to the world, even if it is on the level of not engaging with road rage after a stressful and crazy encounter, or smiling and engaging a store clerk, even after waiting in line. We walk a Bodhisattva path of shining light in dark spaces and living with compassion-in-action.

13. Consciously enjoy this Earth walk with compassion-in-action as a main motivator. Do you notice a difference?

_____

_____

_____

_____

_____

_____

_____

_____

_____

14. Is there anything you would like to add right now?

_____

_____

_____

_____

# Summary of Chapter 2

## Energy Anatomy

Please reflect upon this section of energy anatomy structures including the True Mirror, human energy field, subtle bodies, and chakras.

_____

_____

_____

_____

_____

_____

_____

_____

_____

_____

_____

_____

_____

_____

Are there specific areas of intuition or "the clairs" you wish to heighten? How will you do this?

_____

_____

_____

_____

_____

_____

_____

_____

_____

_____

_____

_____

_____

_____

_____

_____

_____

Reflect on the ways you keep in contact with your spiritual self.

_____

_____

_____

_____

_____

_____

_____

_____

_____

_____

_____

_____

_____

_____

*We are Divinity made flesh. The process of incarnating is perfect and magnificent. We are perfectly imperfect and magnificent!*

# Chapter 3

# Energy

# Systems

# *Introduction*

## Human Instruction Manual

We are energy beings. And, we have an energy systems or drivers in place. The last chapter reviewed our energy anatomy. This chapter reflects upon the systems that drive our physical incarnation.

A well-known joke is that it is too bad human beings don't come with an instruction manual. The better joke is that we do! It is written inside, not only in our multidimensional DNA codes, but in our heart, our manifestations, even in our very cells. This chapter looks at various parts of our instruction manual.

As we are multidimensional beings, there are many layers driving incarnation. We reflect upon a number which impact our Lightworker identity and work.

## Chapter 3 Overview

Traditional Theories of Motivation, section 9, lightly covers conventional theories of what drives us, according to the best minds and experimental research for the last 100 + years, including family patterns and identity struggles. We also look at trauma, toxins and addictions and how they drive the personality.

Abraham Maslow's Hierarchy of Needs is highlighted. His Hierarchy is a well-known theory and one of the only models to capture more of a human be-ing than just the biological, social and psychological.

We spend only a short time in the psychological landscape and begin moving into higher, more esoteric drivers which might have influence upon us as Lightworkers.

The Law of Attraction, is highlighted in section 10. This is known as the Universal Law and as you work more consciously and creatively with this subtle magnetic attraction model, you will see why it is known as a universal law! Enough attention cannot be paid to the Law of Attraction in our lives!

We cover a number of attraction exercises from Abraham-Hicks' body of work and end with a 40 Day Abundance Plan. I also include a Lightworker Light Ladder for us to work with every day to lighten our internal landscapes and help them transform into daily clarity and joy.

Engines as Soul Patterns continues an upward momentum into multidimensionality with an overview of soul contracts, soul families, karma, completion of karma, and release of eternal vows, detailed in section 11.

The final section, 12, covers the New Physics of Consciousness. There is so much new, esoteric information available to us. One of the most scientific and scintillating is information imparted through Kryon and Lee Carroll.

In his groundbreaking work, Kryon/Carroll discusses many new drivers in this new energy. According to their perspective, 2012 marked the halfway point between the precession of the equinoxes. The precession is based upon a cycle of the Earth wobbling on its axis, like a top, and circling around the galactic equator. This activity has been described by Newton and many ancient civilizations.

Completing one full turn around the galactic equator takes approximately 26,000 years. We are in the middle of this important celestial time period of being in synch with the galactic equator, which heralds in an important esoteric transition. According to Kryon and others, the "galactic alignment zone" is said to occur with a window of + or – 18 years from 1998.  2012 is the midpoint and this is what the Mayans might have been calculating with their Long Count calendar. But, as we have seen, a calendar is meant to be turned at the beginning of the next year and the Mayans intended a turn, not an end. We just interpreted their calendar from a doomsday perspective.

Looking at this auspicious galactic cycle from a higher consciousness, consider the changes that have come about from 1994 – 2012 including the fall of communism, rise of technology, cell phones, social media, wifi, alternative medicine, climate change, organic food and ecological awareness to mention a few. Although we focus on negative global changes, there are currently 123 democracies out of 192 countries!

The midpoint of this 26,000 year galactic cycle was 2012 and we are only a handful of years past the midpoint. Let's all relax and trust in this larger cycle!

The precession, or transition time will continue until 2030. And, at that point, we will be beginning a new cycle of 26,000 years, measured galactically. So 1994 – 2030, give or take, is the 36 year window of change, with 2012 as the midpoint. Why 36 years? I have no personal answer on that number, but Kryon references the period of monthly changes for astrological signs, which seems 'normal' to us. Galactic time is longer. In fact, as we move more starbound, he mentioned we will counting time as 'rev's' or galactic revolutions rather than earth revolution (day and night) or solar revolutions (1 year).

We end this section with engines of the new physics of consciousness including mining the Akash, death, rejuvenation, destiny path, quantum doorways and for the adventure and joy of it all.

EnJoy!

# Section 9

## Traditional Theories of Motivation

What drives us to act? Why are some people driven to succeed in life and others are not? Motivation is the energy to act, and the strength to see it through, even with challenges. Researchers in psychology, sociology, education, and, especially business all have developed theories of motivating people. We call motivation 'energy driving systems'.

There are a number of basic theories of motivation including instinct or innate, inborn motivations such as a baby knowing to cry to get attention. Examples of drive reduction is wanting to get rid of hunger or thirst. Arousal theory emphasizes wanting stimulation and activity. Psychoanalytic theory, based upon Freud, allows for two basic unconscious drives, life or death or what will increase our success vs what will keep us alive longer?

## Maslow's Hierarchy of Needs

Maslow's theory of motivation is well- known in psychological, and now economic fields, although not necessarily the most researched. Abraham Maslow theorized there is a hierarchy of needs and only when a lower level has been satisfied can a person move to the next level.

His theory is based upon a pyramid shape with the 1st level at the bottom and 5th at the top.

5th level – self actualization, reach our highest potential

4th level – self esteem, achievement, competence, respect

3rd level – belongingness and love

2nd level - safety and security

1st level – physiological needs of food, shelter, clothing

In the 1960's Maslow added a 6th level, the top tier, to his theory:

6th level – self transcendence, peak experiences, mystical, beyond self

Tellingly, psychology texts and papers have refused to modify or amend his hierarchy for the past 50 years. Mainstream institutions and models of reality have their biases and filters as we individuals do, and the 6th level of transcendence is beyond their worldview.

Also, a second interesting complexity is that people are known to have drives towards self-actualization and self-transcendence even when their lower needs are not met. So, rather than theorizing a pyramid shape of motivational drivers, with the necessity of completing one step before attempting a higher run, a more fluid and flexible pattern is needed.

As Lightworkers, we move within all 6 layers, but have a strong pull towards self-actualization and, especially, self-transcendence.

1. Where would you place yourself on Maslow's hierarchy of needs?

_____

_____

_____

_____

_____

_____

2. Have you needed to have lower steps met first before moving on?

_____

_____

_____

_____

_____

_____

# Family and Generational Patterns

Family and generational patterns, including ethnic, culture, social class, birth order, career choices, and other identifying patterns, are researched extensively within psychology and sociology. Each of these patterns can be strong.

Patterns can be conscious or unconscious energy drivers for us throughout our lifetime. Many people live in 'survival programming' as humans have been subject to subsistence living for thousands of years. I encourage you to delve deeply within your generational inheritance and come up with positive, survival strengths and patterns handed down to you. You are here because your ancestors have survived. Untold numbers of lines have died out over the millennia, and yours has survived unto you. Find the strengths, even if they look or are negative.

For example, you may have been taught to be fearful and not risk getting hurt. Although this fear holds you back, the most generous we could say is that your ancestors learned, the hard way, that caution and precaution were good survival strengths. Honor this pattern, then shift out of it. It takes effort, but that's what we Lightworkers do! This is our area of expertise!

1.  Choose one or more of your identifying patterns and trace their motivating forces in your life:

## Factor 1:

_____

_____

_____

_____

_____

## Factor 2:

_____

_____

_____

_____

_____

_____

Factor 3:

_____

_____

_____

_____

_____

_____

Factor 4:

_____

_____

_____

_____

_____

Factor 5:

_____

_____

_____

_____

_____

_____

2.  Are there any patterns you have discerned that you wish to complete, or change?

_____

_____

_____

_____

_____

_____

_____

3.  What are some of your family's survival strengths and skills?

_____

_____

_____

_____

_____

_____

_____

_____

# Trauma, Toxins, and Addictions

Other powerful engines of our habits and choices are driven by circumstances which have the possibility of diminishing our joy over a lifetime. Many Lightworkers come from trauma. The difference is that Lightworkers heal the trauma and move forward in their lives, vibrating wholeness and serenity. People do not know how to heal trauma and instead are encouraged by some professionals and others to carry these scars as identity definers ("incest survivors", "alcoholics", "abusers").

Addictions seem ubiquitous in this time and culture. Derived from Latin ('to assign') we develop dependencies, habits, ways to handle our fear, anxiety, pain, numbness.  There are legal, illegal, everyday, and surreal addictions ranging from chocolate to mood elevators to meth. These can be powerful drivers in our life, and also powerful initiators of guilt, shame, self-loathing, fear, and humiliation.

4.  List some common addictions that you notice in people and perhaps in yourself. What are they driving away?

_____

_____

_____

_____

_____

_____

5.  Do you identify with a trauma as your hero journey story? Are you ready to release that false identity and step into Lightworker identity?

_____

_____

_____

_____

_____

# Section 10

## LAW OF ATTRACTION IN ACTION!

### *"That Which is Like Unto Itself Is Drawn"*

The Law of Attraction is one of the most important understandings to having a fulfilled life. Much has been written about it lately; the most clear, understandable, and inspirational writings and channelings are by Esther Hicks and Abraham.

Being familiar with the Abraham-Hicks body of work is invaluable! Her information and vibratory knowledge of the law of attraction is the highest I know. There are books, CD's, videos and workshops available and I recommend you familiarize yourself thoroughly with her model.

We might think we understand law of attraction but it is an extremely subtle system! It is not only what we say, or what we think, but it also takes into account what we feel which then equates to our 'vibrational offering'.

As referenced in *Ask and It is Given*, the process is as follows:

1. We ask for something,

2. It is immediately given to us, placed in our 'escrow',

3. We vibrate in resonance close enough to attract it into our life experience.

Sounds simple, as is her quote that it is as easy to manifest a castle as it is a button. But, how many castles, or, for that matter, buttons, have you consciously manifested lately?

Time to dive into this fundamental Law and to work our way through some of her basic exercises.

1. How much do you know about Law of Attraction?

_____

_____

_____

_____

_____

_____

2.   Give an example of when you consciously used the Law of Attraction:

_____

_____

_____

_____

_____

3.   Give an example of when you unconsciously used the Law of Attraction:

_____

_____

_____

_____

_____

_____

4.   What do you want to draw to yourself at this time?

_____

_____

_____

_____

_____

_____

5. What is a vibrational set point?

_____

_____

_____

_____

_____

_____

_____

6. What is your vibrational set point in the situation above you wish to bring into your life at this time?

_____

_____

_____

_____

7. How are you going to attract it in?

_____

_____

_____

_____

_____

_____

8. How are you going to release resistance to letting it in?

_____

_____

_____

_____

_____

_____

_____

_____

_____

_____

## Fun with Law of Attraction

Following are some of my favorite Abraham-Hicks exercises and underlying structures of law of attraction. These include the Emotional Guidance Scale, Segment Intending, the Focus Wheel, and 'Wouldn't it be nice if...'

As Abraham-Hicks states, our emotions are indicators of our vibrational frequencies. Each emotion, or each step of her *Emotional Guidance Scale* of emotions, has a rising vibrational frequency. Emotions are indicate how aligned we are we our Source Energy of love, value, and purpose. The top emotions on her scale are joy, knowledge, empowerment, freedom, love, and appreciation. The bottom emotions are fear, grief, depression, powerlessness, and despair. Ranges of emotions scale from 1 – 22 depending upon the amount of relief one feels as one moves up the scale towards empowerment.

To someone who studied psychology and counseling for decades, this small scale was breathtaking and life changing for me. Nowhere were we ever taught that emotions scale vibrationally in this manner, and that it is about ability and responsibility to move ourselves up the ladder. Such clarity!

Please take time to read, in entirety, *Ask and It is Given* by Abraham-Hicks. Work with the *Emotional Guidance Scale* in your own life. Determine for yourself the power and simplicity of moving up the scale.

The *Emotional Guidance Scale* ranks 1 – 7 with positive emotions and 8 – 22 with varying degrees of negative emotional states. For our purposes as Lightworkers, I have enlarged upon the Emotional Guidance Scale and the Scale of Consciousness by David Hawkins to create the *Lightworker Light Ladder.*

This Light Ladder is similar to both systems as the emotional states are vibratory in scale. It also incorporates 11 as a master number and ranks 11 higher frequencies and 11 lower vibrational frequencies.  As with the other scales, the names are not the important feature. The importance is the feeling of relief as you move up the scale and the feeling of disempowerment as you find yourself dropping down the scale.

# Lightworker Light Ladder

1. unbounded joy, feeling of transcendence, inner connection
2. expansive sense of Self, Self-love, Self-worth
3. compassion-in-action, dedication, devotion
4. passion, creativity, excitement, integrity
5. appreciation, gratitude, creative silver linings
6. feeling in-the-flow, empowered, service
7. inspired, centered, authentic
8. listening to inner guidance, inner peace, confidence
9. hope, calm, patience, inner strength, determination
10. contentment, self-determination, seeing possibilities
11. acceptance, faith, optimism
12. boredom, distractions, light addictions
13. tiredness, sadness, confusion
14. doubt, disappointment, uncertainty
15. blame, worry, pessimism
16. discouragement, denial, pride
17. anxiety, disappointment, regret
18. revenge, anger, fear
19. hatred, rage, panic
20. jealousy, guilt, apathy
21. shame, depression, unworthiness
22. despair, misery, hopelessness, grief

9. Working with the Lightworker Light Ladder, determine your step today. Are you OK with this step? Would you want to go higher? How would you do this?

_____

_____

_____

_____

_____

_____

_____

_____

_____

_____

_____

_____

_____

_____

_____

_____

_____

10. Work with the Lightworker Light Ladder every day for this week. Chart your ability to, determine your step, and your ability to feel joy today.

Day 1

_____

_____

Day 2

_____

_____

Day 3

_____

_____

Day 4

_____

_____

Day 5

_____

_____

Day 6

_____

_____

Day 7

_____

_____

11. What tools are you using to move up the scale?

_____

_____

_____

_____

_____

_____

_____

_____

_____

_____

12. Do you notice any patterns of where and why you might drop lower on the Lightworker Light Ladder?

_____

_____

_____

_____

_____

_____

I love when Abraham-Hicks states that only you know if anger is an appropriate emotion for you, as it depends upon your placement on the scale. If you were vibrating lower than anger, then it is appropriate. If you were vibrating higher than anger, then you have dropped. No judgment! Anchor in and move up again.

13. Recount an incident when you dropped lower on the Lightworker or Emotional Guidance scale. How did you move up again?

_____

_____

_____

_____

_____

_____

_____

_____

_____

_____

_____

_____

14. Do you believe you can live every day in levels 1 – 11 on the Lightworker Light Ladder?

_____

_____

_____

_____

## Exercise #1 Intent vs. Reaction

In *Ask and It is Given,* Abraham-Hicks details a wonderful exercise which they call 'Segment Intending'. This practice helps us to consciously create the day or situation in front of us by 'pre-paving' your emotional pathway. This process helps us to be deliberate in our focus and in the thoughts we are choosing. Not sure you are choosing thoughts? Then, put your conscious attention on what thoughts will make you feel good, and continue to focus on those.

They suggest you start with small segments of time and put an intent on that segment. Preparing to leave the house – intend it to be a calm experience. Getting in the car is another segment. What are you intending for the drive? Driving on your route is another segment. Reaching your destination is yet another segment.

It is more effective to break our day into small segments in which we intend what we want. We need practice! There are worthwhile results in intending for larger periods though. Gentle your way through this practice.

15. Read the section on Segment Intending, process #11. What do you think of this exercise?

_____

_____

_____

_____

_____

_____

_____

16. Recount your experiences with segment intending today. Try to consciously work this exercise all week.

_____

_____

_____

_____

_____

Day 1

_____

_____

Day 2

_____

_____

Day 3

_____

_____

Day 4

_____

_____

Day 5

_____

_____

Day 6

_____

_____

Day 7

_____

_____

## Exercise #2  Spin to Appreciation

In *Ask and It is Given*, Abraham-Hicks describes process #17, The Focus Wheel, as a way to pivot from where you are currently attracting or thinking about a person or situation to where you want to be. This, again, is a seemingly innocuous and easy exercise, but, as all her work, it is subtle and extremely powerful.

Esther Hicks documents details about how and why this process works, or why we hold certain 'truths' about our life circumstances. "He will never change."  "My boss is horrible."

Draw a wheel with 12 spokes on it. Similar to a clock number from 1 – 12. Start in the middle with the end result: "I love and honor my body." Start at 1:00 (the book mentions starting at 12 but that feels counter-intuitive to me but start where it feels right for you). On the spoke write a statement that is easy for you to align with. Example, "Bodies are designed to function well."

Then work your way around the wheel, adding incrementally to each statement as you progress towards 12:00. This is a smaller version of Esther Hicks' magnificent Rampage of Appreciation. You can read her rampages in *Ask and It is Given*, and there are samples of her speaking them on YouTube.

This process looks and feels like a merry-go-round in a park. You start running slowly around the circle, then pick up speed. Match the speed, jump on and enjoy the ride!

I have tried this exercise and recommend it highly.

17. What are some issues or situations you wish to feel better about?

_____

_____

_____

_____

_____

_____

_____

_____

_____

18. Draw a Focus Wheel below on an issues. Write the 12 ascending affirmations and jump on (vibrationally). Did you notice a shift or release in your thoughts? Did you notice a shift or release in the situation?

## Exercise #3  Lighten Up

I recommend you try ALL the exercises in *Ask and It Is Given*, but this last one we will try together is a soft and fun one. Instead of using logic or beating ourselves up to try and achieve a goal (getting a new job, a new relationship, losing weight, getting out of debt, etc.) we design affirmations, and vibrational offerings, which soften our thoughts, help us to release resistance, and to attract in more of what we desire.

Try Process #12, "Wouldn't it be nice if...?" in *Ask and It Is Given*.

19. Write a page full of soft 'wouldn't it be nice if...?' affirmations for an issue you wish to work on:

_____

_____

_____

_____

_____

_____

_____

_____

_____

_____

_____

_____

_____

_____

_____

## Exercise 4:  Confrontation- From the Outside In

Another view of The Law of Attraction is from the outside in. Look at the 3D manifestation in your life. Is it what you want? Lovingly and compassionately recognize that your creation is a manifestation of your vibration. It is crystal clear. To change 3D you need to recognize, honor, and then change your 'vibrational offering'. Sounds simple, but it is confronting and deep-core work.

20. Look at an area of your life that you wish would change, for example your finances, relationships, health, home life, etc. Choose one area. Sit with yourself in light meditation and consider that you are vibrating to attract in the situation the way it is operating in your life. Breathe in that vibration.  Now, how can you lighten your vibration to attract in more of what you do want, not what you don't want?

_____

_____

_____

_____

_____

_____

_____

_____

_____

_____

_____

_____

_____

_____

## Exercise 5  Abundance

*The Abundance Book*, by John Randolph Pierce, is a great way to align law of attraction vibrations around money and abundance. He describes money as:

- **M**y

- **O**wn

- **N**et

- **E**nergy

- **Y**ield

There are 10 affirmations which describe our ultimate relationship with money and abundance, such as "God is lavish, unfailing abundance."  "Money is not my supply. No person, place or condition is my supply."

These 10 affirmations are repeated once a day, 4 times,  for a 40 Day Abundance Plan. It is wonderful to work together, sending Reiki to each other and to our abundance as a group. We will choose a day to start. Each day, repeat the phrase and reflect upon it. You will find your core beliefs about money and abundance very easily with this program. Your meditation and uplifting vibration about money and abundance is life affirming and life changing.

21. What is your relationship with money and abundance?

_____

_____

_____

_____

_____

22. Write a short reflection or observation for each of the 40 days below:

_____

_____

_____

_____

_____

Day 1:

_____

_____

Day 2:

_____

_____

Day 3:

_____

_____

Day 4:

_____

_____

Day 5:

_____

_____

Day 6:

_____

_____

Day 7:

_____

_____

Day 8:

_____

_____

Day 9:

_____

_____

Day 10:

_____

_____

Day 11:

_____

_____

Day 12:

_____

_____

Day 13:

_____

_____

Day 14:

_____

_____

Day 15:

_____

_____

Day 16:

_____

_____

Day 17:

_____

_____

Day 18:

_____

_____

Day 19:

_____

_____

Day 20:

_____

_____

Day 21:

_____

_____

Day 22:

_____

_____

Day 23:

_____

_____

Day 24:

_____

_____

Day 25:

_____

_____

Day 26:

_____

_____

Day 27:

_____

_____

Day 28:

_____

_____

Day 29:

_____

_____

Day 30:

_____

_____

Day 31:

_____

_____

Day 32:

_____

_____

Day 33:

_____

_____

Day 34:

_____

_____

Day 35:

_____

_____

Day 36:

_____

_____

Day 37:

_____

_____

Day 38:

_____

_____

Day 39:

_____

_____

Day 40:

_____

_____

23. What is your relationship with money and abundance?

_____

_____

_____

_____

_____

_____

_____

_____

_____

24. What are some of your core beliefs which you have released?

_____

_____

_____

_____

_____

_____

_____

# Section 11

## Soul Patterns as Engines

Moving up the vibrational scale of motivation and drivers, we now cover seven different possible engines which can drive or motivate our lives. These include soul contracts and soul families, karma, karma completion, releasing eternal vows, passions, sense of mission, and 'watching-the-wheels'. These seven engines are discussed below with reflection space for you.

## Soul Contracts and Soul Families

Visualize Spirit in non-physical choosing a lifetime for its own purposes. This is done with a team of Guides who offer advice and guidance on soul contracts and life tasks. Each Soul's has choices before re-incarnation.

Sound imaginative? *Journey of Souls, Destiny of Souls* and *Life Between Lives* by Michael Newton, PhD are fascinating books that describe the between-life times we, as Souls, experience. Newton is a psychotherapist and hypnotherapist, rigorously trained in not believing in an afterlife. However, after inadvertently regressing a client to a between - life experience, he began to focus on this area. After hypnotizing and hearing the same story from many clients, Newton wrote the series mentioned above. And, he does believe in life between lives now.

If we regard life between lives, with Souls choosing life details (gender, family, society, culture, time period, trajectories, contracts) as a possible working model of reality, let's consider how Soul Contracts could impact us.

From the lens of Soul Contracts and Soul Families, spend some time reflecting upon some of your possible contracts. These would be higher level perspectives on the people in your life and the situations that seem 'accidental' or beyond our choice. For example, take an important person in your life and look at them from the highest perspective you can, affirming they are Beings of Love and Light who travel with you for lifetimes, who love you dearly, and who you love dearly. This would hold true even those who may have hurt you unbearably in this lifetime.

The same lens applies to circumstances and situations that may have traumatized or plagued you. Instead of asking (correctly from a personality level), why this happened to you, the soul contract lens asks you to consider, using your creativity and compassion, a possible higher perspective.

For example, perhaps you have suffered abuse, physical, mental, or sexual as a child or young adult. Perhaps this occurred from the so-called loving family member you pray you never meet or incarnate with again. How to move from the very real 3D perspective, with your actual past time line?

A higher perspective could be that you, as a Soul, (not as the personality who was birthed), chose to work on bringing light to dark areas of child abuse so that they can be healed and released. Taking it even higher, breaking this pattern of abuse would not only be healed in your family lineage, sparing your descendants from continuing this pattern. As a Lightworker, healing this pattern could then be set into the global arena, changing the consciousness of the planet. This perspective and service I call 'Stringing Pearls'.

A last note about Soul Families. It is sometimes challenging to consider, but, unless you are balancing or completing karma with this person, then only those Beings who love you dearly are willing to incarnate and hurt you so that you may set healing energies on a wide scale. Yes, this is a very high perspective. But, it is just as much a possible reality as a perspective that you are unconsciously saddled with a horror for no reason. Taking it even higher, when you break this pattern of abuse, you not only heal it for yourself but you heal it also for your family lineage, sparing...

1. Consider working from a Soul Contract and Soul Family perspective. Review all the important people in your life from birth. What could be the Soul Contracts?

## Soul Family/Soul Contracts:

_____

_____

_____

_____

_____

_____

_____

_____

## Soul Family/Soul Contracts:

_____

_____

_____

_____

_____

_____

_____

_____

_____

Soul Family/Soul Contracts:

_____

_____

_____

_____

_____

_____

_____

_____

_____

_____

Soul Family/Soul Contracts:

_____

_____

_____

_____

_____

_____

_____

_____

_____

Soul Family/Soul Contracts:

_____

_____

_____

_____

_____

_____

_____

_____

_____

_____

Soul Family/Soul Contracts:

_____

_____

_____

_____

_____

_____

_____

_____

_____

_____

_____

2. What is your perspective on Soul Contracts and Soul Family?

_____

_____

_____

_____

_____

_____

_____

_____

_____

_____

_____

_____

_____

_____

_____

_____

_____

_____

# SoulAnge Lineages

As Lightworkers, we are graced to descend from not only DNA lineages or past life adventures and wisdoms, but also we align with Angelic or Soul Ray lineages. These descend from the 'I AM Presence' down through the dimensions to our present life and our shining personal gifts.

Chapter 9, section 29 lists SoulAnge Lineages for past Apprentices. Add yours!

_____

_____

_____

_____

_____

_____

_____

_____

_____

_____

_____

_____

_____

_____

_____

# Karma

Karma is a Sanskrit word meaning cause or action. Do you remember being young and wondering why certain things happen to certain people? It can seem that good things happen to bad people, and bad things happen to good people. Sometimes, it seems that people get what they 'deserve' and other times they seemingly get away freely with no justice or repercussions.

In pondering injustice, social and political, in Christian dogma we are taught that everything is sorted out after death. People will be judged after their one and only lifetime (by God or St. Peter at the pearly gates) and go to heaven, purgatory, or hell.

Buddhist scriptures detail a story of a young person asking the Buddha why there was injustice in the world. He answered that karma, or the law of cause and effect, was in action and that we reincarnate to balance this karma. This driver of life engines, or motivations, also answers the question why some people have innate skills and aptitudes, many times not associated with genetics or early learning environments.

Although I was not trained to believe in reincarnation, seeing the misery and suffering of people around me, and being told to wait till after death for judgment and punishment/rewards never seemed to be as just or logical as reincarnation. Interestingly, there are many Bible scholar books which state that Jesus and early Christians also adhered to the idea of reincarnation and karma, but they were written out by the councils which decided the official Christian dogma. This was done for political power, economic rewards, control of the population, and the perils of moral laxity ("I don't have to give alms to the church now, I can always do it next lifetime").

These are two separate models of reality, and we live in a culture that adheres mainly to the one lifetime/judgment- by- others after death. Most of us in America have been raised with this model, even if we were not brought up within any religious structure. And the truth of this model is that it is really not 'us' who reincarnates. The physical, genetic, individual with the specific time/cultural stamp is completely unique and does not replicate again. The 'us' that reincarnates is the Soul essence, so it is a very subtle issue.

A third common model in the west for the past 300 years is the scientific worldview – one lifetime. No life after death. No higher consciousness, no working with cause and effect or innate moral codes. A harsher offshoot of this third model is survival of the fittest. The weak deserve the little they get.

A fourth common model of reality is the one chosen by agnostics. "I don't know." This could also be stated by some, "I don't care. I'll find out when I die. Or not. Makes no difference. "

And, the truth of this last model is that we all don't really know and will find out after we die. But, not to care? There's a lot at stake from that position.

3.  What model were you raised and entrained to believe in? Do you still believe in this model of reality or did you change your belief?

_____

_____

_____

_____

_____

_____

_____

_____

4.  If you changed models of reality, what caused you to change? Do you still live with doubt?

_____

_____

_____

_____

_____

_____

_____

_____

_____

_____

5.  What do you think of reincarnation and karma?

_____

_____

_____

_____

_____

_____

_____

6.  Do you consider yourself an 'Old Soul"? What does this mean to you?

_____

_____

_____

_____

_____

_____

_____

_____

## Karma Completion

For those who work within a karma/reincarnation worldview, some think karma is 'bad' and that we will have to pay for things we think, say and do. Others believe karma is just a natural driver or life motivator, a law of the universe, and that it is a teacher.

Kryon was the first person who brought to my attention that we can set the intent to complete our karma.

> *"In Kryon Book One (1993), I spoke about something that innate is responsible for. I said, "It's time to drop your karma." Karma is energy carried with you as a result of past-life experience, pulled forward through the veil into a reincarnate body. It is an energy of unfinished business. That's karma. It's real, and it was needed in an older energy.*
>
> *It's in the DNA and innate governs it. So when I told you to drop your karma, I told you that you must talk to your body and talk to your cells. When you do that, say, "I am done with the energy of the past. I drop my old karma. I move forward."*
>
> *We told you to use pure intent."*  (www. Kryon.com/ Portland 2015)

According to Kryon and Lee Carroll, karma was necessary for 'older energy' but not for these shift times. You set the intent and drop your karma.

The challenging part is that without your driver or map, you might feet adrift for a while as you determine what to do and where to go. An interesting enigma!

7.  Are you interested in the construct of dropping your karma?

_____

_____

_____

_____

_____

_____

_____

_____

## Releasing Eternal Vows

This possible engine of motivation involves a reincarnation perspective and one that is common for Lightworkers. If you consider the possibility of past lives, then you may have had monastic or religious lifetimes. This life path was a very common one for many people for thousands of years, and especially for those of us who pursue higher wisdom paths.

In these past monastic lives, religious often took eternal vows of 'poverty, chastity, and obedience'. And these 'eternal' vows can be in existence now, driving us into experiencing a lack of money, relationships or self-autonomy. Most people resolve one or more but it could take time (lifetimes) to allow ourselves the freedom from these (eternal) vows.

8.  Do you feel that you are being hampered by a past life eternal vow?

_____

_____

_____

_____

_____

9.  If so, would you want to release from the vow? You can set the intent that "I now release myself fully and completely from a vow of _____".  I claim my authority as an eternal being of love and light to enjoy (lavish abundance/ loving relationships/ self-determination and freedom).

_____

_____

_____

_____

_____

_____

_____

## Passions vs. Fears

Programming runs deep within us, and many times we are unaware of the origins or even existence of our core programming.

Sometimes we know, on a deep soul level, that we are meant to be .... (an artist, a mother, an Olympic contender, an author, a healer, a social activist, etc.) For some people there are deep passions that run our lives from our earliest memories and we might face enormous odds or pressures to achieve or release them, but they stay as important drivers, whether we attain them or whether they haunt us as what might-have-been.

At the opposite end of this love/passion spectrum is a deep programming of fear. Sometimes we feel the need to be invisible and to hide who we are and what we are. This driver can be overwhelming and interrupt our deepest longings, having us swing from desire to fear in a lifetime loop.

From the fear perspective, many Lightworkers have been on the forefront of the arc of justice, peace, tolerance, and wellness lifetime after lifetimes. And there are immeasurable costs and penalties involved. Reading history we learn that many spiritually pioneering people were tortured, killed, ostracized, shunned, and humiliated. Spiritual choices have cost dearly, life after life. Ever have dreams of being martyred? Have a particular fear of burning or drowning? Or, perhaps you 'just' have a fear or hesitation to express that you are an energy healer, afraid to present who you really are, even to loved ones you trust and live with?

The core drivers of passions and deep fear runs deep and can be powerful engines in a life.

10. Do these core drivers touch you in any way?

_____

_____

_____

_____

_____

_____

_____

_____

_____

11. What are some of the deep passions you have had since your earliest years?

_____

_____

_____

_____

_____

_____

12. Do you carry deep fear about being humiliated or shunned for your energy or Light work, even though you know you are surrounded by support?

_____

_____

_____

_____

_____

_____

_____

_____

_____

_____

_____

## Sense of Mission

You may know people who seem to be drifting along with the tides, reacting to whatever life presents, with no sense of direction, 'wasting time, doing time' as John Lennon describes. Lightworkers feel a sense of mission, purpose, and an urgency to fulfill this mission, even though most don't know what that might be.

The sense of urgency of mission, or even the dual sense of urgency/unknowingness often causes anxiety and a sense of missed opportunity.

'Souls in Service' are those who choose to incarnate on Earth even though they have wisdom beyond current Earth vibration ranges. It is a blessing to have (you!) souls in service here. It is a blessing to have (you) souls in service walking, talking, breathing higher vibrations, raising the set range for everyone. That is mission enough! If you choose, add on other fun mission-adventures.

13. Do you feel a sense of mission driving you? Is this a good feeling or a conflicted one for you?

_____

_____

_____

_____

_____

_____

_____

_____

_____

_____

_____

_____

14. Do you know what that mission is?

_____

_____

_____

_____

_____

_____

_____

_____

_____

Beings of Love and Light often express that there is a sense of mission and purpose to life on Earth – and that one mission is to enjoy this life and enjoy the adventure of being in physical.

15. Breathe in this mission and feel the relief. Can you align with this as your main mission?

_____

_____

_____

_____

_____

_____

## R & R Lifetime

We can read about the lifestyles of fabulously wealthy and playful millionaires and billionaires who spend thousands on champagne, yachts, and parties and judge that they are wasting money, time, or resources. From a soul perspective, however, they may be doing exactly what they came to do – have lavish, abundant fun.

It is hard to judge another's choices, and it's also hard to judge our own. The most generous and creative story we can consider is that a soul may have toiled under tremendously harsh conditions for many lifetimes, eking out a subsistence life. Perhaps they starved in many lifetimes or had to watch their children starve. A fun soul contract might be for them to choose this lifetime to have a rest and relaxation lifetime with no worries, only fun and over-the-top excess. Then, with some healing accomplished to soothe jagged nerves, they might get right back to work again in a next (challenging) lifetime.

Although written with a smile to you, this could be the case and it teaches us not to judge. Even resting and relaxing can be a soul contract as well as wasteful extravagance. Let's keep our minds and hearts focused on our journey!

# Section 12

## New Physics of Consciousness

Kryon, an Angelic being of 'magnetic service' is channeled by Lee Carroll. Lee is a fascinating author and workshop presenter and I strongly recommend your attending one of his many offerings. His website, www.Kryon.com is a wealth of esoteric information. There are many transcribed speeches, audiofiles, and a substantial question-and-answer format which you can spend hours enjoying.

For this section on motivational energy engines we will reflect upon six esoteric engines of accessing all of you, death, and rejuvenation through Innate Intelligence, destiny path, quantum doorways and for the joy and adventure.

## Access All of You

An interesting consideration, Kryon says that we have every skill and every ability we have accumulated through every lifetime in our Akash, which is located within our quantum DNA. And, we can access this information! He calls this attribute, 'Mining the Akash'. Giving a personal example, Lee says he was a very introverted sound engineer before channeling Kryon. He hated being around people and he hated speaking to groups. Along came this new lifestyle of global presenter and Lee 'mined his orator Akash', bringing forth the qualities and skill set of a speaker. He now travels and speaks worldwide, seemingly enjoying every minute.

This engine is an esoteric one, based upon intent, and allows us to consciously access inner skills we might not have in this current lifetime. We drive the engine consciously by choosing to 'mine the Akash' or plumb our depths to pull out those skills and abilities.

1. Do you have a dream or a skill you wish to access from your past lives or Akash?

_____

_____

_____

_____

_____

_____

_____

_____

2. Set a prayer of intent to allow those skills and abilities to come effortlessly to your consciousness. "Ask and it shall be given unto you."

_____

_____

_____

_____

_____

_____

_____

_____

# Death

Death is not usually seen as a driver of consciousness, although people who face their death say that living is more potent and enjoyable when viewed from that angle. Drivers or motivations can also come from desires to complete 'bucket lists'.

Kryon says that in an old energy, our normal way of amassing wisdom and understandings, adding to our personal Akash, is to die. We grow, learn, die, and assimilate the wisdom.

> *"In order for you to graduate, pick up the wisdom, and move forward into a higher spiritual consciousness in the next life, you need a short and productive life. Then you reincarnate with that wisdom. The faster the learning cycles are, the higher potential there is for the planet to awaken into a higher vibration – spiritual evolution... In an older consciousness, this became the "engine of enlightenment."*

However, in this new energy (since 2012), it is no longer necessary to die to assimilate our wisdom on a soul level. Thus, we can set the intent to rejuvenate and live longer, healthier, more vital lives.

## Rejuvenation through Innate Intelligence

> *"Suddenly in 2012, you passed the marker (as measured by the precession of the equinoxes)... Your DNA is starting to evolve.... Longer lifetimes are the key to the planet's evolution... Old souls of this planet, awaken! Awaken to a new process and a new life. You can double your lifespan and more."*

Imagine living a strong, vital, healthy, purposeful life until... 80? 90? 100? There are super centenarians living today who are said to live until 120's. Can you visualize living vibrantly until 120's? In the Bible many were said to live hundreds of years. In channeled writings, beings live thousands of years. Our life expectancy ranges from high 70's to low 80's depending upon gender, ethnicity and country. Kryon is encouraging an engine of rejuvenation to keep our wisdom intact and continue our work for much longer lives! Double our lifespan?

3.  Do you have a strong desire to live a long life?

_____

_____

_____

_____

_____

_____

## Highest Destiny Path

This engine of incarnation is one connected to Soul in Service as it details a life in which we consciously intend to walk our Highest Destiny Path. What would that look like?

Vision a life path with many turns and curves, organically moving like a river cutting its ribbon-like path through landscape tapestry. After leaving Source, there are youthful areas of playful bouncing and trouncing, restful curves, possible blockages and stagnation, heart-pounding rapids, cascading waterfalls, even dry bed trickles which wait for melting snows from on high. With mature rivers we find gentler flows and wider banks, and, finally, an emptying into the sea.

Within this playful archetype, envision spaces when there are multiple ways for the river to flow. In our lives, we can intend to choose the highest destiny path. And this drives our life moments.

4.  If you choose, intend to walk your Highest Destiny Path. Affirm this daily.

_____

_____

_____

_____

_____

_____

## Quantum Doorways

Derived directly from quantum physics, working with quantum doorways as a driver of our life path is one that helps dispel regret, remorse, and recrimination. We are multidimensional beings in a multidimensional reality and we are just learning to grasp the potentials.

Understanding that there are many possible future realities, draw a half circle on a piece of paper and put a number of doorways, perhaps 3 – 4 for an issue or memory you are struggling with.

For each doorway, consider an alternate life path wherein you made a different decision or had a different life circumstance. For those you would dearly like to consider, put a Hon Sha Ze Sho Nen, the distant sending symbol, on the doorway, open the door and step through.

Feel what it is like to be in an alternate reality. Bring the lightness, healing energies and wisdom back with you into this reality.

Working with quantum doorways is an advanced healing method and one that can profoundly influence the drivers of this 3D reality for you. Never got to tell a loved one you are sorry or that you love them? Do so through the quantum doorway. Beating yourself up for something you said or did in the past? Go through the doorway and do it differently. Releasing grief, guilt, shame, humiliation is liberating and allows for a very different vibratory set point in your life.

5.  Try setting up and walking through a quantum doorway. How do you feel afterwards?

_____

_____

_____

_____

_____

_____

_____

_____

_____

## For the Joy and Adventure

A final driver of our life choices is ... for the joy and adventure. This is such a simple driver, and yet one that is very profound for us. We have been entrained for this entire life, and others as well, to be humans do-ing not humans be-ing. And, especially, not human be-ings just enjoying the adventure of being alive on planet Earth, reveling in the physicality and abundance of options.

Angels, as Light Beings, encourage us by affirming there is nothing we can do or feel or think that we are not loved unconditionally, recognized, and honored. Some channeled writings state that humans are held in awe by Spirit as we choose to come and engage with and emerge in this physicality, enduring tremendous high's and low's, all without knowing our home base, who we are, or why we are here. For us, as explorer humans, this is all part of the joy and adventure!

6.   Are you able to feel the joy and adventure of being alive?  How often?

_____

_____

_____

_____

_____

_____

_____

# *Summary of Chapter 3*

## Energy Systems

Take a moment to reflect on the Human Instruction Manual from theories of motivation, the universal law of attraction, engines as soul patterns and the new physics of consciousness.

_____

_____

_____

_____

_____

_____

_____

_____

_____

_____

_____

_____

_____

_____

What areas are you excited by?  What insights have you received?

_____

_____

_____

_____

_____

_____

_____

_____

_____

_____

_____

_____

_____

_____

_____

_____

_____

_____

Are there specific areas or patterns you notice that you wish to change in some way?

_____

_____

_____

_____

_____

_____

_____

_____

_____

_____

_____

_____

_____

_____

_____

_____

_____

What areas are you most comfortable with / grateful for?

_____

_____

_____

_____

_____

_____

_____

_____

_____

_____

_____

_____

*My love, you wish to capture the stars?*
*They burn through your hands on their flight from*
*your heart.*

# Part 2

# Energy Healing Work

# Introduction

# Energy Healing Work

Part 2 covers the mechanics of our energy healing work by offering basic tools and techniques that many energy healers use in their practice.

Chapter 4 is a collection of various energy healing tools used by many in the field. We will go over these tools in our monthly group meetings and you are encouraged to take notes and reflect on how they work for you.

Chapter 5 is an overview of inspirations, lenses, and filters of reality. There is space to reflect upon and discuss luminaries in our fields of interest and to capture notes and reflections of your Apprentice level energy training class.

Chapter 6 offers basics on preparing for a healing session with clients including preparation, conducting a session, and clearing after a session.

EnJoy! This is what we've incarnated for!

# Chapter 4

# Energy

# Tools &

# Techniques

# Energy Tools & Techniques

This chapter allows us to spend more time with energy tools and techniques, which can enhance our Lightwork.

The tools and techniques described below are a sampling of those used in my practice. We are all guided to activities which resonate with us vibrationally. There may be others which you currently use or which you feel guided to use and feel free to add them to the end of the list.

Use your inner guidance system and your discernment when choosing and using tools!

For example, I once went to a workshop on using pendulums. There were so many beautiful types of pendulums and we practiced getting a 'yes' and a 'no' answer by watching the pendulum swing clockwise, counterclockwise, or straight up and down.

I asked the pendulum if I could buy the one I was trying.

Answer, "No".

Not one to give up easily, I asked was there another one I could use. Answer, "No".

I went through a series of questions making sure I got 'yes' answers. I concluded by asking,

"Could I just buy one to have around?"

Answer, "No".

I was finally convinced.

I know practitioners who use pendulums a lot in their practice to get information, and they do wonderful work. Others use body talk and other biomechanical means to circumvent conscious thought in their healing practices, and they do wonderful work. However, those methods don't resonate with me personally. They might with you. Trust your inner messages. Be discerning. You don't need many tools – just the right ones for you.

## Purpose of energy tools and techniques

Tools provide an opening for us to go deeper into the experience and provide an opening for clients to go deeper into the healing session. They can be very effective in clearing our space, and creating boundaries and protections. Finally, certain tools are wonderful in increasing the power of our light work and helping us gain higher perspective on situations and issues.

YOU are the tool!

Don't be overly intrigued by or convinced that a certain tool or technique affects healing. They don't really. You are the tool and you consciously choose to work with different vibrational offerings that resonate with you. These resonators bring you a feeling of inspiration, relief, blessings, and allow your intuition to expand.

You are really the only tool you need. We are vibrational beings in a vibrational universe, intending to bring about a vibrational shift of consciousness within the larger Mandalic

Consciousness of All There Is. Don't be fooled into thinking that any particular tool itself holds answers. Or that astrological or numerical structures hold answers. Or that rituals hold answers. You are the one with the consciousness to incarnate and do this work. YOU!

And, similarly, you do not heal nor do your tools heal your clients. They open themselves to the universal healing energies and step up into release, empowerment and healing. Perhaps you are a part of their optimism, trust and relief, but they are the ones who step up vibrationally.

The real power behind energy tools and techniques is that they help you feel more 'you'. They allow you to suspend limited thinking and unique, solitary boxed confinements. They open you to wider vistas and possibilities of who you really are. They might also make you smile, breathe, or delight you in some way. They are treasures and personal. They also can hold vibrational energies so be sure to clear your space and your tools frequently.

## Multidimensional qualities

Energy work is an 'art' as well as a 'science' and, although ancient, it is still barely being accepted in our society (and, maybe, in our lives). The wave of energy work has barely begun to rise, no less crest. Part of the enigma and challenge surrounding energy work is that it is perceived and interpreted differently and sometimes uniquely by practitioners and by clients.

Some of the items listed below can be seen as a tool, others as a technique. Others can be both tool and technique. Some of those listed below are described in different chapters in the manual. There is crossover and interconnectedness. Don't try to overanalyze the details. Multidimensional attributes aren't easily linearized or quantified.

Relax. Trust your inner messages and guidance. Discern 'who' is guiding you – your mental tapes, messages locked in from childhood, fear based thought projections, gut instinct, true inner guidance, or channeled wisdom. There are so many whispers within!

Enjoy your unique perspective and practice your craft until you feel confident in your ability to gather wisdom within for your own Lightwork and highest destiny path!

# Chapter 4 Overview

We will invest time in each of these tools and techniques in our group training, private sessions and energy healing circles. They are presented alphabetically with a short essay and follow-up reflections.

## Sacred Energy Tools and Techniques

1. Angel and Oracle Cards
2. Affirm the Best
3. Altar/Sacred Space
4. Ask for Help
5. Calendar
6. Clear, Align, and Balance Chakras Daily
7. Colors, Clothing, Jewelry
8. Crystals, Rocks, Grids
9. Daily Meditation
10. Essential Oils
11. Flower Essences
12. Gemstones and Elixirs
13. Give Thanks
14. GRACE!
15. Music, Singing, Chanting
16. Open Angel Musculature and Wings
17. Poetry
18. Prayer
19. Send Reiki Daily
20. Sing Angel Names
21. Smudge, Clear Air
22. Wear Reiki Symbols

EnJoy the adventure!

# Section 13

## Sacred Energy Tools & Techniques

### *Angel and Oracle Cards*

Healers have made use of wisdom cards, runes, tokens, sticks and even bones for thousands of years. They are ways of bypassing our linear, left brained logic, and our cause and effect perspectives on reality. They increase our intuitive skills, our narrative work, and our inner connections. Synchronicities abound when using cards! We enter the realm of quantum entanglement and gain higher perspectives on everyday issues. No question is too mundane.

There are many different types of cards:

* ✳ Angel, Archangel, Saint cards: these are positive messages of healing and empowerment

* ✳ Tarot cards: there are many versions including angel, mermaid, animal, fairy, fairytale, and mythic (to name a few) as well as traditional playing cards; tarot cards give a fuller reading of both light and challenges

* ✳ Affirmation cards: these cards have a picture and affirmation and can focused on one or more areas such as mastery, health, abundance, and relationships

* ✳ Artistic cards: these cards have only visual messaging with no words; the reader is left to uniquely interpret the meaning

* ✳ Specialty cards: there are so many interesting and unique cards including Mayan, galactic, fractal, light coding and more

If you are drawn to this Light tool, ask for guidance on choosing a deck. Work for a while with that deck until it becomes known to you.

When asking for guidance or more information, shuffle the cards while forming your intent. You may also want to breathe upon the deck, smudge it, or do Reiki on the deck to clear it. Ask your question(s) and then choose a card from the top, after cutting the deck, or spread the cards out, fan-like, and with your non-dominant hand, choose a card.

In class we will go over practice with various card decks, with reading meanings, and with ways to lay out the cards. As with all tools, practice make it easier and more fun.

EnJoy working with your new 'friends'!

1. Do you have regular decks? Why did you choose that deck? How did you choose that deck?

_____

_____

_____

_____

_____

2. After trying a few decks, and seeing various ways to read the messages, how do you feel about using decks in the future?

_____

_____

_____

_____

_____

3. Did you receive a 'perfect' answer or message for your question?

_____

_____

_____

_____

_____

_____

## Affirm the Best

It takes practice and feeling our way to find the affirmation that moves us a step higher vibrationally, not too many steps ahead and certainly not behind. Write, sing, dance, doodle your way through daily affirmations.

Get a notebook and write pages of the same affirmation, from 3 perspectives: I, you, and he/she. For example,

I, Lorelynn, love to eat foods that make my body feel great.

Lorelynn, you love to eat foods that make your body feel great.

Lorelynn loves to eat foods that make her body feel great.

In this way of speaking from 3 perspectives, you are speaking to your unconscious mind to unwind old tapes of eating foods that might be comfort foods, but that don't align with who you are now.

Always stay in the present (I will …. Means, not today!). Stay positive. Be compassionate and kind.

Keeping a detailed journal helps us to focus. *Daily DeLights Engagement Journal* has a page a week dedicated to affirmations.

4.  What affirmation would you like to work on? Try it for a week. How do you feel after your week of practice?

_____

_____

_____

_____

_____

_____

_____

_____

_____

## Altar/ Sacred Space

It is so enriching, nourishing and inspiring to have sacred space around us. In my home and office I love to work with a combination of sacred, whimsy, and seasonal themes. It brings a sense of home, generations, and joy to me.

Within a heartfelt environment, having a sacred space for your energy tools is a wonderful addition. You might place crystal, grids, flowers, sacred objects, inspirations readings and more in this space.

Sacred space serves many functions, including a 'portal' of allowing us immediate access to our inner worlds.

EnJoy creating space around you which invites you in!

5.  Do you have a sacred space in your home?  What do you have in your space?

_____

_____

_____

_____

_____

6.  Would you like to add anything to your space?

_____

_____

_____

_____

7.  What colors are in your sacred space?  What messages do they bring?

_____

_____

_____

_____

## Ask for Help

I cannot emphasize enough the importance of asking for help! This is a free will planet and we need to choose to ask for help, otherwise our Helpers, Guides, and Guardian Angels honor our choice to go it alone.

Not sure who to ask for help from? That is not a problem. Just say, "Please help me!" You do not need to direct the call. If you do enjoy calling upon specific Beings of Love and Light – then have fun doing so.

Archangel Michael is great for safety and courage

Archangel Raphael is wonderful for healing requests

Jesus, Mary and the Magdala, Tower of Strength are power intermediaries as are Buddha, and Quan Yin, the Goddess of Compassion.

8.   Make a choice to call upon Higher Beings every day. Do you notice a difference in your life?

_____

_____

_____

_____

_____

_____

_____

_____

## *Calendar*

It is a wonderful addition to your daily round to have inspirational calendars to allow a quick reminder or intent to start your day. I have a perpetual Angel calendar in my bathroom, so I can read while I look in the mirror and prepare myself for the day. My husband has a Zen calendar in his bathroom, which offers another perspective on wisdom. And, in my kitchen, I have a perpetual Law of Attraction calendar to help me remember what it is I am attracting today. Each year, I turn the perpetual calendars around and start again, never seeming tired of the messages!

9.  Do you have quick, easily accessed fonts of wisdom, such as perpetual calendars around you?

_____

_____

_____

_____

_____

_____

_____

_____

_____

_____

_____

_____

## Clear, Align and Balance Chakras Daily

It is our responsibility to clear, align and balance our chakras daily!

Have fun working with your chakras. They hold tremendous information for you and are interdimensional 'portals' into your Inner Child, your Hero's Journey, and your karmic completion.

There are many wonderful ways to clear your chakras:

- Use Cho Ku Rei on each chakra
- Put Reiki on each chakra
- Put oils your hand and motion them in front of your chakras
- Meditate on each of your chakras
- Use guided visualizations for clearing and aligning chakras
- Use affirmations for each chakra

EnJoy working with your energy transducers!

10. Do you have a favorite way to clear and balance your chakras?

_____

_____

_____

_____

_____

_____

_____

_____

_____

11. Is there one chakra in particular that seems to need more attention from you?

_____

_____

_____

_____

_____

_____

12. Ask to 'see' your Inner Child. What chakra are they currently 'living' in?

_____

_____

_____

_____

_____

13. Are you enjoying the Expanded Chakra meditation?

_____

_____

_____

_____

_____

## *Colors, Clothing, Jewelry*

Putting intent into our clothing, colors and jewelry all help to step us into a multidimensional state as we do our Lightwork. Color is frequency and has a huge impact upon us and upon our clients. Choose your daily colors in joy, balance, and harmony.

Invest in sacred jewelry and clothing that feels wonderful so that you are wrapping your body in symbols, design, and elements that uplift and inspire you and your clients.

Have fun and enJOY wearing frequencies that enhance the True You to peek out during your days! Use the Law of Attraction to magnify to you the resources you would like to add to your colors, clothing and jewelry!

14. Take a look in your closet and drawers. What colors are you drawn to wearing?

_____

_____

_____

_____

_____

15. Do you need to add to your color repertoire?

_____

_____

_____

16. How do you feel when you wear 'your' colors? Which colors make you smile, inside and out?

_____

_____

_____

_____

_____

17. Do you have special jewelry that brings out your inner sparkle and helps with your Lightwork?

_____

_____

_____

_____

_____

_____

18. Are you happy with your clothing?  What would you like to change?

_____

_____

_____

_____

_____

_____

_____

_____

_____

_____

_____

## Crystals, Rocks, Grids

Crystals, gems, rocks and other nature gifts (acorns, flowers, feathers, etc.) are truly gifts to us from our Earth Mother.

They help ground and protect us (especially rocks, mud, onyx, agates and hematite).

They help balance our mental and emotional fields (especially rose quartz and amethyst).

They are great for magnifying our purposes (white quartz).

And, they open us to higher dimensions (citrine, lapus lazuli, smoky quartz and celestite are favorites of mine).

The Crystal Reiki Grid is taught in Reiki Master and advanced levels. This grid works for your intents and once in motion can last weeks and months.

EnJoy working with the magnificent gifts of Gaia!

19. What crystals, rocks and gems do you work with?

_____

_____

_____

_____

_____

_____

20. What have you found from your work with these tools?

_____

_____

_____

_____

_____

21. Draw the Reiki Crystal Grid below. What have you found from your work with the Reiki Crystal Grid?

## Daily Meditation

Meditation is a practice, a gift, an embrace, and an energy technique for Lightworkers. Meditation brings us into the sanctuary within. It brings us peace, connection, wisdom, and ageless information.

There are many different types of meditation – explore, be guided, and try ones that work for you. Breath work is a main type of meditation for me, as is walking my dog, drinking afternoon tea, writing in a journal, and showering! Every moment can be a breath-by-breath mindful, heartful meditation – at least that is something we can aspire to!

As Lightworkers, connecting to the Wise One within, and to our divinity, to Source Energy is an important part of our life. It can be as long as a breath or as short as an hour a day. Build a meditative lifestyle to nourish you. EnJoy each breath!

22. Do you have a daily meditative practice?  What does it look like?

_____

_____

_____

_____

_____

23. If so, how long have you practiced this routine?

_____

_____

_____

_____

_____

_____

24. Is there anything else you would like to change in your practice?

_____

_____

_____

_____

_____

_____

25. If you don't have a current practice, how can you start and take small steps?

_____

_____

_____

_____

_____

_____

26. How do you feel on the days you meditate and the days you don't?

_____

_____

_____

_____

_____

## *Essential Oils*

Oils have been in use for sacred ceremonies, and for everyday living, for thousands of years. There are many wonderful therapeutic grade oils available today. Young Living ™ and DoTerra ™ are two well-known, high quality therapeutic oils.

I have been using oils as energy tools for almost 20 years and find them essential in my practice. There are so many ways for you to use oils:

✓ diffuse the oils to cleanse your healing and practice space

✓ spray a water bottle with oils on the Reiki table before and after a session

✓ spray on your hands before and especially after a healing session

✓ spray oils with symbols in your room instead of smudging

✓ spray oils with symbols in the ceiling corners for protection

✓ put the oils directly on your chakras

✓ smell the oils to oxygenate yourself and for clarity, wisdom, energy

Young Living oils have many single blend oils and also numerous blended oils which you can use on yourself for healing, balance, and empowerment. Try different oils and add to your sacred tool kit.

Some essential oils are lavender, peppermint, Thieves, and lemon. Other wonderful 'friends' are Abundance, Harmony, Peace and Calming, Gentle Baby, Magnify Your Purpose, Into the Future, Exodus, Release and Trauma Life.

EnJoy the adventure of discovering the wonders of therapeutic oils!

27. What is your experience using therapeutic grade oils?

_____

_____

_____

_____

_____

_____

_____

_____

28. Do you have favorite 'go-to' oils?

_____

_____

_____

_____

_____

_____

_____

_____

29. How could you integrate oils in your life?

_____

_____

_____

_____

_____

30. How could you integrate oils with clients?

_____

_____

_____

_____

_____

## Flower Essences

Flower essences are another wonderful tool for Lightwork.

They are vibrationally based, like homeopathy, and can be blended uniquely for clients and for various conditions.

There are many wonderful high quality flower essences on the market today. Two of my favorites are from the Flower Essence Society (FES) in California and Perelandra brands.  Both are exquisite. FES sells a desk reference guide to using their oils, which is invaluable. Perelandra has unique combinations, such as soul ray essences, viral/bacterial/fungal essences, and many beautiful rose essences.

Using flower essences enhances greatly your intuitive abilities!

The following is a basic guide:

- ✓ Consider what area(s) you wish to work on
- ✓ Read through the various essences you own to see which ones 'pop out'
- ✓ Prepare your bottle by putting 2/3 filtered water, little less than 1/3 either liquor (I use Peach Schnaps) or apple cider vinegar
- ✓ Put approximately 1 -4 drops of various essences in your dropper bottle
- ✓ Keep a list of essences on the back of a 3 x 5 index card
- ✓ On the front of the index card put the date and a few affirmations to help integrate the essences into your, or your client's, fields
- ✓ Put a label on the bottle with the date and a title (Moving Forward, Balancing in Joy, Forgiveness, etc.)
- ✓ Take a few drops each day. Put them in a glass of water and sip throughout the day. Put a few drops in a bath.
- ✓ Read your affirmations daily to integrate mental, emotional and spiritual

As flower essences are vibrational, it is more effective to frequently resonate with the essences rather than take one full dropper a day.

EnJoy the adventures of working with flower essences!

31. What essences and issues are you working with during this Apprenticeship?

_____

_____

_____

_____

_____

_____

_____

_____

_____

32. What differences are you noticing when taking them?

_____

_____

_____

_____

_____

_____

_____

33. Feedback from clients, family, friends or observations with your animal companions?

_____

_____

_____

_____

_____

_____

_____

_____

34. How could you integrate flower essences with clients?

_____

_____

_____

_____

_____

_____

_____

_____

_____

## Gemstones & Elixirs

Therapeutic grade gemstones are very exciting and empowering to work with. We are fortunate to have a world class therapeutic gemstone storefront in Portland, OR. Michael Katz, an originator of Gemisphere, has written numerous books about gemstones, from the gem's narrative perspective. I highly recommend his work.

Often elixirs are made from gemstones and they are vibrational medicines much like flower essences. Refer to the use of flower essences when using gemstone elixirs.

EnJoy Gais's bounty!

35. What have you experienced with gemstones or elixirs?

_____

_____

_____

_____

_____

_____

_____

_____

36. Do you notice a difference when wearing, holding or taking them?

_____

_____

_____

_____

_____

_____

_____

## Give Thanks Daily

It is one of our major strengths, as Lightworkers, to be able to find, affirm, and truthfully feel (resonate) thanks during all kinds of 'weather'. We find the silver lining in clouds, we rejoice at the power of storms. It sounds paradoxical, but sometimes it is easy to forget to give thanks when the sun is shining and it is a beautiful day!

It takes tremendous creativity, insight and 'breakthrough thinking' to find the good in life situations and to not only say we are grateful, but to really <u>feel</u> grateful. Keeping a detailed journal helps us to focus. *Daily DeLights Engagement Journal* has a page a week dedicated to gratitudes.

37. How comfortable are you with daily Gratitudes? List a few.

_____

_____

_____

_____

_____

_____

38. What one thing can you do differently to increase the power of thanks and positivity in your life today?

_____

_____

_____

_____

_____

_____

_____

## GRACE!

*GRACE!* is an acronym for

- ✦ **G**  Ground  (physical)

- ✦ **R**  Root     (physical/generational)

- ✦ **A**  Align    (mental)

- ✦ **C**  Center   (emotional)

- ✦ **E**  Elevate  (spiritual)

- ✦ **!**  Alchemically pop into our community  (energetic)

*Daily DeLights* Engagement Journal, Book 1 of the Tools for Lightworkers Series details many examples of the GRACE! process and allows you to work daily to bring yourself into alignment and harmony.

39. Are you working the GRACE! process?  How is it going for you? Do you notice any patterns?

_____

_____

_____

_____

_____

_____

_____

_____

_____

_____

_____

## Music, Singing, Chanting

Enough cannot be said about bringing your vocal instrument – you! – to your healing and mastery Lightwork practice. We are each vocally unique and allowing ourselves the opportunity to sing and chant opens our chakras, especially the 4th and 5th chakras, and enhances our inner connection.

Be discerning about your music environment

Chant vowels to get yourself into a sacred space

Sing songs or symbols or affirmations when out walking or driving a car

Sound is a creative, emotive, cathartic, inspiring and altering experience. Sound healing is an art, an intuition guide, and a privilege. Bring your song and your voice out to the world!

EnJoy swimming in the ocean of sound!

40. What types of sound healing are you enjoying?

_____

_____

_____

_____

_____

_____

41. How do you feel after singing?

_____

_____

_____

_____

_____

_____

42. How do you feel after chanting vowels?

_____

_____

_____

_____

_____

_____

_____

43. How can you bring more music, sound and chanting to your practice and your Lightwork?

_____

_____

_____

_____

_____

_____

_____

_____

_____

_____

## Open Angel Musculature and Wings

These unique Angelic musculature exercises are wonderful! They expand us and also free us to be more of an angelic nature, which is one of unconditional love and acceptance, for ourselves, for others, and for life situations.

For the first exercise, put a drop of an essential oil on your shoulder blades and flex them up and down, visioning your wings opening and fluffing out. Visualize your wings unfolding, like an origami peace crane, until they are way above your head and more than arms' length wide and long. Use your fingertips to motion the height, depth, and width of your wings. Envision colors, white, or iridescent /pearlescent color on your unique wings. Do this every morning after you clear your chakras and put on your Reiki symbols.

A second exercise follows from the first, but this time walk around the room for a few minutes, balancing out your new walk with large wings surrounding you, adding to your personal presence and earth walk.

Another exercise is for your clients as they lay on the Reiki table. At the end of a healing session, and as part of the closure, motion your hands from their shoulder blades upward past their head. Hold this vision for your client of their Angelic nature while you close the session.

EnJoy your Angel flights!

44. How do you like opening your wings every day?

_____

_____

_____

_____

_____

_____

_____

_____

_____

_____

45. Do you feel a difference on the days you work your Angelic musculature and the days you don't?

_____

_____

_____

_____

_____

46. Try singing your Angelic name and opening up your wings together. How is this experience?

_____

_____

_____

_____

_____

_____

47. Can you more easily identify yourself as someone who walks with Angels, talks with Angels, sings with Angels, and does Angel work?

_____

_____

_____

_____

_____

## Poetry

Sacred, inspirational poetry has the ability to help you transcend daily challenges and stories, and transport you to a higher vibratory state in the space of a few minutes.

Inspirational books are wonderful as well. Intend to gather information to uplift or inspire you, or put Reiki on the book, and then open a page and read. My challenge is that it is hard for me to stop reading. Poetry, by nature, is short and sweet as well as delicious. It is an 'amuse bouche' for our soul.

Daniel Ladinsky's body of work is exquisite. *Love Poems from God* offers devotional poetry from eastern and western sources. Find your inspiration! Ride the waves of transcendence and join the bhakti dance (of devotion). You will feel the love embrace!

48. Who are some of your inspirational poets?

_____

_____

_____

_____

_____

_____

_____

_____

_____

_____

_____

_____

## Prayer

Prayer is a practice, a gift, and also an energy tool for Lightworkers!

There are many ways to pray, ask for guidance, or ask for help, even if it is as simple as …. "Help!" There is not even a need to direct the prayer to anyone in particular. In this free will incarnation, help is available but we need to open and ask for it. Otherwise, the intent is that we wish to handle this on our own resources – which is honored and perfectly fine.

Daily prayer, reading a line of inspired poetry, or requesting help is an active form of reaching out to the Universe. Reiki is another active form of reaching out. Meditation is a form of surrendering within. These three practices work together in our lives harmoniously, synergistically, and weave around and within us wonderful channels of communication.

EnJoy this daily connection!

49. Do you pray every day?  How?

_____

_____

_____

_____

_____

_____

_____

50. Do you notice a difference on the days you pray and the days you don't?

_____

_____

_____

_____

_____

_____

_____

51. What do you normally pray for?

_____

_____

_____

_____

_____

52. Do you have an inner world of Beings you pray to?

_____

_____

_____

_____

_____

53. Is there anything you would like to add to your practice?

_____

_____

_____

_____

_____

## *Send Reiki Daily*

Sending Reiki is a practice, a gift, and also an energy tool for Lightworkers! The more we practice, the more we get to experience, and also the more we are called to do!

After you have been attuned to Reiki 2, distance sending, use the Hon Sha Ze Sho Nen symbol and send daily. Perhaps you have a morning meditation routine and send Reiki at that time. You might also, like me, enjoy sending Reiki at night. I frequently wake up at night and, instead of being upset that I am awake, I use the time to send Reiki to my family, to those who have asked and are in need, to life circumstances, and to you!

EnJoy lighting up your life as a working energy healer every day!

54. When do you normally send Reiki? Do you have a routine in place?

_____

_____

_____

_____

_____

_____

55. 5Have you noticed a difference in your skills after sending every day?

_____

_____

_____

_____

_____

_____

## Sing Angel Names

Singing in your SoulAnge angelic lineage is a blessing and a gift to us from our Higher Selves!

This personal and unique song is the song of your I AM lineage as it has manifested down a particular Soul Ray essence into the wonderful presence of YOU in this 3D manifestation.

Singing your Lineage will open a 'portal' for you to step through into a clearer, more concentrated dialogue with the higher, wiser You that incarnates from life to life.

EnJoy this precious song!

56. How do you feel when you sing your angelic song?

_____

_____

_____

_____

_____

_____

_____

_____

_____

_____

_____

_____

_____

## Smudge, Clear Air

Smuding, or burning sage, is an ancient tradition, most recently used by indigenous Native tribes to clear, sanctify, bless, and protect your physical space. Most often sage is burned, but cedarwood, lavender, sweetgrass, palo santo sticks, frankincense and copal are also burned. They are put in a ceramic or alabaster bowl, in a stick, or wand. The smoke is only burned for a few moments and, according to Native tradition, it is good to open a window or door during smudging.

Incense has also been burned for thousands of years, although now much incense has other ingredients added which are often harder to assimilate.

At times it is imprudent to burn sage, especially in public or commercial spaces, and spraying oils diffused in water is a good remedy.

Candles have also been used for thousands of years to focus attention, send to healing intents, and bring a sense of the sacred to your space. Again, like incense, candles are primarily made with harder to tolerate ingredients. Beeswax is a good alternative. Non-burning candles are a possible substitution, although they don't carry the same enjoyment as flame.

EnJoy the ancient art of smudging!

57. Do you smudge?  What ingredients have you used in smudging?

_____

_____

_____

_____

_____

58. Do you notice a difference when you smudge and when you don't?

_____

_____

_____

_____

_____

_____

## *Wear Reiki Symbols*

This is a basic energy tool. 'Wear' your Reiki symbols every day by any of the following: draw on your body, on your palms, in your car, in your home or office. Vision them, blow them on your breath, or try singing your Reiki symbols.

The symbols are basic energy glyphs, like the beginning of a sacred geometry language, the Language of Light. They are representations of the forms behind reality and we can easily access this vibratory and consciously creative dimension by intending and kinesthetically moving the symbols through our fields.

The 6 major Usui Reiki symbols are:

✴ Cho Ku Rei – divine wisdom and power, protections, blessings

✴ Sei He Ki – mental and emotional healing, balance and empowerment

✴ Hon Sha Ze Sho Nen – sending healing, balancing and empowering energies through time, space and dimension

✴ Dai Ko Mio/Dai Koo Myo – the yin and yang of Mastery

✴ Serpent of Fire –gentle integration of energies

As you remember, you need to be attuned to these symbols for them to become activated and work in your energy fields.

For those who have been attuned to advanced energy healing glyphs, choose variations to work with. This includes Om, the Master symbol for Karuna Reiki and Language of Light, and the wonderful Living Fractal of Light symbols. With over 80 glyphs to enchant us, still, the first three are essential for everyday use.

Put Cho Ku Rei in the shower when you get up, in the car before you drive, and in the ceilings of your office and home. Also – and most important – draw a large Cho Ku Rei on your body and smaller ones over each chakra to keep your field boundaried and protected and to clear, align and balance your chakras every day.

EnJoy wearing your symbols every day!

59. Draw and wear your symbols and reflect upon those days when you do and do not put your symbols on first.

60. Is it getting easier to remember to wear your symbols?

_____

_____

_____

_____

_____

_____

61. How else do you use sacred symbols every day?

_____

_____

_____

_____

_____

_____

62. Do you have other favorite symbols?

_____

_____

_____

_____

_____

## *Your Personal Energy Tools and Techniques:*

63. What additional energy tools and techniques do you work with?

_____

_____

_____

_____

_____

_____

_____

_____

_____

_____

_____

_____

_____

_____

_____

64. What daily practices not mentioned do you currently enjoy in your daily lighting up?

_____

_____

_____

_____

_____

_____

_____

_____

_____

_____

_____

_____

_____

_____

_____

_____

# Summary of Chapter 4

## Energy Tools & Techniques

Please reflect upon this section of sacred tools and techniques. Are there specific areas you wish to add to your tool kit? Which ones resonate with you more strongly? Which ones do not?

_____

_____

_____

_____

_____

_____

_____

_____

_____

_____

_____

_____

_____

_____

_____

_____

Have you noticed a change in your intuitive gifts with daily practice of energy tools?

_____

_____

_____

_____

_____

_____

_____

_____

_____

_____

_____

_____

*We have the ability and the responsibility to step between dimensions and create space for healings to occur.*

# Chapter 5

# Energy

# Trainings

# Energy Trainings

Throughout our Apprenticeship, we will review many types of inspirations from master teachers who match our understandings and who encourage our training in the energy field. Wisdom is available to those who ask. There are a number of inspired writings which underpin the Apprentice program and these authors are reflected in Section 14, Inspirations, Lenses, and Filters of Reality.

We have many filters in place since our earliest years. As Esther Hicks/Abraham points out, we are vibrational beings in a vibrational universe and we perceive through vibrational senses. Consensus reality takes shape. Sometimes it's hard to see the forest for the trees. As energy healers we work at fine tuning our filters so that we can detect the subtle messages emanating from within. We also work at removing ourselves mentally, emotionally, physically and spiritually from socially filtered messages of fear, doom, intolerance or confusion.

You are asked in this section to reflect upon those who inspire you and to continue researching the materials you are guided to. It's wonderful to share in the wealth of inspired offerings!

The second section, 15, offers a reflection of the energy training classes that you were attuned for this Apprenticeship. Investment for each level is one year.

Let's bring together many of our tools, techniques, and trainings!

# Section 14

## Inspirations, Lenses, and Filters of Reality

For camera buffs, filters are put over lens for protection against dust and fingerprints. They are also used to sharpen focus and often help to block, reduce, or diffuse light. What about multiple, over-layering filters?

Although we work hard to assure ourselves that we are correctly perceiving situations and people, we are many times unaware of the various filters that have been put in place since our earliest years.

Have you recently spent time observing a toddler being 'socialized' at home and in pre-school or kindergarten? It's very instructional! Continue to observe elementary, middle and high school. The filters of what it means to be a 'good' student, a 'good' person usually revolves around obedience, managing boredom and sedentary environments, and learning parameters in an absolute norm setting versus a relaxed, generational, cooperative natural setting.

Families set rules of what it means to live successfully. Religion and science entrain us to their structures of reality. Professional programs build consensus thinking and ostracize pioneers. Work cultures demand adherence to unique norms. Media is ubiquitous. Politics is dysfunctional, with constituents existing in a bubble of like-mindedness. There is an effusion of anxiety and fear. The list of filters is large and growing.

Children are not racist, sexist, bigoted, or lacking in empathy for those who are fragile before they have been 'socialized'. Although scientific folklore seems to indicate that we are competitive by nature and survival of the fittest rules, that is not true in the animal kingdom or in human civilizations throughout history. We survive, and thrive, with cooperation. When empathy and compassion are not conditioned out of us, we are a kind and caring social group network. But that's hard to believe in a society where we see people live and die in poverty, homelessness and pain all around us, and our social training and politics tell us those people deserve their fate – just walk on by. Conscious capitalism cannot come too soon!

It's hard to recognize when our filters drop into place over our eyes, but our hearts are always free. If it constricts our hearts, then filters have dropped down, no matter who is talking.

## Crystalline Lenses

It takes discernment for us to continue to clear and improve our view of what is the truth behind 3D swirling times. And it takes practice. And creativity. And courage. And asking for guidance and help. Rather than allow ourselves to be at the mercy of media makers and their agendas, we have the ability and responsibility to remove outmoded filters. Instead of blocking, reducing or diffusing light, let's use filters to help us see more and more light and love!

We are so blessed that there are many inspired texts and readings for us to bathe ourselves in. During this program you will be asked to read certain books and website materials. You are also asked to share knowledge that you use as a foundation in your life, as a bridge to a higher level, or as divinely guided information.

1. Look at your personal library, shelf, or computer screen. What books do you have / cherish? (They don't necessarily have to be 'spiritual' – Spirit talks to us through infinite media!) Who are some of your favorite authors?

_____

_____

_____

_____

_____

_____

_____

_____

_____

_____

_____

_____

2.  What are some of the best films you have seen?

_____

_____

_____

_____

_____

_____

_____

3.  What songs inspire and uplift you?

_____

_____

_____

_____

_____

_____

_____

_____

_____

_____

_____

_____

4. Who are some of the people whose lives have inspired you?

_____

_____

_____

_____

_____

_____

_____

_____

_____

5. Have you tried contacting any who have transitioned and dialogue with them? With Reiki 2 training, we are able to go between time, space and dimension!

_____

_____

_____

_____

_____

_____

_____

_____

_____

_____

# Recommended Reading 1

## *Ask and It Is Given*, Esther and Jerry Hicks and Abraham

There is no clearer channel of information on the Law of Attraction than Abraham and Esther Hicks. There are numerous books, CD's, videos, and workshops to help us more clearly understand and work the Law in our lives. Her 'Rampage of Appreciation' is magnificent. If you have not ever seen Esther and Abraham, I strongly recommend it!

6.   How did you like this book? How does it relate to your life right now?

_____

_____

_____

_____

_____

_____

7.   What did you think of the Emotional Guidance Scale?

_____

_____

_____

_____

_____

_____

_____

8.  What is an example of moving your vibrational set point?

_____

_____

_____

_____

_____

_____

9.  Are you finding it easier to monitor your emotional states and move up the scale?

_____

_____

_____

_____

_____

10. Are you enjoying 'segment intending'?

_____

_____

_____

_____

_____

_____

# Recommended Reading 2

## Lee Carroll and Kryon books

Another excellent resource I have found is **www. Kryon.com**, offered by **Lee Carroll**. Lee and Kryon have over 13 books on channeled information. His website is very user friendly and you can easily access years' worth of audio and written material.

Another good starting point is presented on the topics page of the website. Listed in alphabetical order, you can scan through multiple questions and topics, gleaning fascinating information from a soul based perspective.

Some of his pioneering insights are on mining our akash, building bridges to innate intelligence, 12 layers of (magnetic, quantum, and biological) DNA, and Earth time capsules. It's fascinating to consider life from a soul perspective!

Enjoy traveling!

11. List below any notes or information that piques your interest from Kryon and Lee:

_____

_____

_____

_____

_____

_____

_____

_____

_____

_____

_____

# Mystics, sages, saints, luminaries, poets, and visionaries

There are so many inspiring resources available to us today!

Some of my favorites are edited by Daniel Ladinsky. He has a genius of translating esoteric information into modern day language, keeping the heart, soul, and humor intact and current. Once Hafiz enters your heart, it is never the same!

Here are sweet soul/love poems for you:

- *I Heard God Laughing: Renderings of Hafiz (2003)*
- *The Subject Tonight Is Love: Sixty Wild and Sweet Poems of Hafiz (2006)*
- *The Gift: Poems by Hafiz (1999)*
- *Love Poems from God : Twelve Sacred Voices from the East and West (2002)*
- *A Year With Hafiz: Daily Contemplations (2011)*
- *The Purity of Desire: 100 Poems of Rumi (2012)*

12. List some of yours!

_____

_____

_____

_____

_____

_____

_____

_____

_____

_____

# Merging the strands of science and religion:

## A unified and quantum consciousness!

There is no need to isolate ourselves into separate camps. Science and spiritual understandings are weaving together with pioneers in both fields. Many decades ago, Pierre Teilhard de Chardin revolutionized the Catholic world with his otherworldly visions. Today's scientists are charting unknown territories in their quest for truth, including a grand unifying theory of the macro and micro worlds. There are visionary writers in archeology, genetics, psychology, chemistry, biology, physics, and sacred geometry.

Some of my favorites are:

- Gregg Braden

- Dean Radin and others from Noetic Sciences

- Bruce Lipton

- Michael Newton

13. Who are some of your favorites?

_____

_____

_____

_____

_____

_____

_____

_____

_____

_____

# Follow your heart....

... and use your discernment when taking in new information, from well known authors and speakers, from channeled writers, from media or the news, even from me.

We have a responsibility to keep our filters of reality clear so we can more effectively and effortlessly see the reality behind 3D and shine our light for conscious and compassionate action.

14. Reflect on your filters of reality, inspirations, discernment:

_____

_____

_____

_____

_____

_____

_____

_____

_____

_____

_____

_____

_____

_____

_____

_____

_____

# Section 15

## Arise Apprentice Energy Training Classes

For this Apprenticeship, you are being trained in one of the six levels below. The next few pages offer you reflection space to capture notes from the classes, inspirations from your attunement, and a fractal curve of your Lightworker Identity.

## The six levels of training are:

*Level 1: Lightworker*
> Offered for those beginning the journey as an energy healer and Lightworker.
> *Reiki 1* and *Reiki 2* classes. Beginning energy healing techniques.

*Level 2: Advanced Lightworker*
> Offered for those who have already received Reiki 1 & 2.
> *Reiki Master class*. Intermediate energy healing techniques.

*Level 3:  Language of Light Healer*
> Offered for those who have already received Reiki Master.
> *Karuna Reiki Master* TM and *Language of Light Healing Master* TM  classes.
> Intermediate.

*Level 4: Advanced Energy Healer*
> Offered for those who have received Level 3.
> *Living Fractals of Light* TM classes. Advanced energy healing techniques.

*Level 5: Etheric Healer*
> Offered for those who have received levels 3, 4 recommended.
> *Spectrum Energetics* TM class.  Advanced energy healing techniques.

*Level 6: Advanced Etheric Healer*
> Offered for those who have completed Level 5.
> *SoulAnge Harmonics*TM.classes. Advanced energy healing techniques.

Energy Healing Class: _____

Date: _____

Notes:

_____

_____

_____

_____

_____

_____

_____

_____

_____

_____

_____

_____

_____

_____

_____

Attunement reflections:

_____

_____

_____

_____

_____

_____

_____

_____

_____

_____

_____

_____

_____

_____

_____

_____

Please note your personal reflections on this energy training class as an enhancement of Lightworker identity:

_____

_____

_____

_____

_____

_____

_____

_____

_____

_____

_____

_____

_____

_____

_____

_____

_____

# Summary of Chapter 5

## Energy Trainings

Please reflect upon this section of energy trainings. What are some of your lenses and filters of reality?

_____

_____

_____

_____

_____

_____

_____

_____

_____

_____

_____

_____

_____

_____

_____

_____

Are you inspired by the recommended readings? Which ones and why?

_____

_____

_____

_____

_____

_____

_____

_____

_____

_____

_____

*We are here as part of an advanced cohort, a 'leading edge of thought'. This is who we are! This is what we do!*

# Chapter 6

# Healing

# Sessions

# Healing Sessions

You have been trained in your energy healing classes about how to give a healing session. This chapter gives you an overall summary of preparation, conducting, and closing a session.

The three phases to conducting a healing include:

Phase 1    Preparing yourself, your client, the environment

Phase 2    Conducting the session by stepping yourself and your client deeper into a multidimensional space for healing and empowerment to occur

Phase 3    Concluding the session by stepping both you and your client back to feeling grounded, safe and vitalized

Section 16 details phase 1, preparation for healing, including preparing yourself, your client and the environment.

Conducting the actual session, phase 2, is covered under Section 17. This includes environmental considerations, Prayers of Intent, and Guided Visualizations. I also include my standard prayer and visualization for you.

Section 18 includes phase 3, closing the session and professional concerns. At the end of Section 18 is a summary page of conducting a healing session.

EnJoy this precious work we are privileged to be a part of!

# Section 16

## Phase 1: Preparing for a Healing Session

There are three main areas to focus upon for preparing to give a healing session:

- ✓ Preparing yourself
- ✓ Preparing the space
- ✓ Preparing the client

## Preparing yourself

In preparing yourself, be sure to allow enough time to bring focus and intent, including cleansing rituals, special clothing or colors, and putting Reiki symbols on yourself. Put the power symbol, Cho Ku Rei, down your body and then put tiny Cho Ku Rei's over each of your chakras. Draw the Master Symbols if you have been attuned for them.

Connect within to your Higher Self, Guides and energies who work with you and with your client. You may choose to meditate, listen to inspired music, chant, or engage in other types of meditative and higher order activities to help you move effortlessly between dimensions. You could also choose one or more Angel or Oracle cards to get a message for the client or the healing narrative.

State a prayer of intent for yourself. Affirm you are a Lightworker, a healer, and that energy work is your craft, your love, your dedicated service. Ask for Guidance and help to intend the Highest and Greatest Good for All. And that means for you, too!

It can take a few minutes to prepare for a session, or it can take hours to prepare. It is up to you! Time is not the major element – You are! Have fun and take things lightly but sacredly as you design ceremony around your preparation.

## Preparing the environment

Preparing the room or healing space is very important. You need to feel comfortable in your sacred space so you can feel inspired and relaxed for the session. This will aid your intuitive insights. Be discerning with your color scheme and decorative touches. But also be true to yourself and your sense of the sacred.

Some people like to design and work in a professional, aesthetic environment. Others are drawn to earthy, goddess themes or religious, sacred figures. Some frame pictures of Reiki masters or Ascended masters. My aesthetic is 'sacred and whimsical'. I love being surrounded by things that make me smile, inside and out.

Keep distractions to a minimum, which might mean turning off phones and ringers. Be sure to have adjustable temperature control and clean bedding. As many people have problems lying flat on their backs, it is good to have an extra pillow or cushion to place under their knees.

Bless and purify the space beforehand with oils, Reiki symbols, or, if appropriate, smudging. Be aware that some clients think sage is marijuana and certain spaces do not allow burning herbs or candles for fire hazards. Also, people are more sensitive to scents of all kinds, so better to be conservative with using scent if you don't know the client's sensitivities beforehand.

Put all the Reiki symbols in the room. Draw a large version of each one of the symbols and motion them into all of the 4 walls, the ceiling and the floor, filling the space completely with – Divine love and wisdom, mental and emotional healing and balance, and stepping between time, space and dimension for healing to occur (Cho Ku Rei, Sei He Ki, and Hon Sha Ze Sho Nen, respectively). If you wish to follow many Native traditions, you would start with the east wall, and move clockwise.

Put the power symbol, Cho Ku Rei in all the 4 ceiling points. This will protect your energy space. Affirm that "We are in protected and safe sacred space".

If you have been attuned with advanced healing symbols, then you might also wish to place those in the room as well. You will feel the difference of a 'charged space'.

## Preparing the client

Preparing the client depends upon whether you know the person or not. For new clients, allow them a few minutes to settle in. I usually ask if they would like some herbal tea or water and I leave the space for a moment or two to allow them privacy to look around and start to feel comfortable in my space. Sometimes they may have rushed to get to the appointment. They could be a little nervous, or overly excited. Some are not feeling well or have other concerns. Reiki goes where it needs to go, and allowing a little breathing space in the beginning can be welcoming.

Give them a brief introduction to Reiki if this is their first session. I normally say that Reiki is like an internal massage – it feels warm and nurturing inside. I mention the touch is very light, and I give them an example on their arm while also assuring that I can just as easily work completely off their body so there is no need for touch at all. The choice is completely theirs.

I inform them that while they are on the table we could talk a little if they like, they could ask questions, go to the restroom, be silent, or even fall asleep. All are perfectly acceptable and common. Laughter is great!

Finally, because I normally say a verbal Prayer of Intent to start the session, I may ask who populates their inner world? Do they have special beings they pray to or would like me to call in for them? Most people appreciate this question, even if they say it doesn't matter. For many, it does matter. As long as the Beings are of Love and Light, I am fine to verbally call in their requests. In the majority of cases it is Jesus, sometimes they align with Angels or a specific Angel in particular, mostly Michael.

Occasionally they wish to call in a Loved One who has transitioned. I will mention them in my Prayer of Intent by name, or generically mention 'Loved Ones of the Light'. If you are open to this type of dialogue from those who love the client, watch over them, and are in communication with them, it is a wonderful and humbling experience. But it is not necessary, so discern for yourself if this is work you wish to do, and then ask for it and practice.

# Section 17

## Phase 2: Conducting a Healing Session

## Environmental Attentions

For the healing session, consider light, rhythmic music which can help settle you into the experience and which can also serve as an ambient noise buffer. Most clients are soothed by the light music as well.

Main songs for me are *Chakra Suite* by Steven Halpern, *Songs of Kuan Yin* by various artists, featuring Deva Premal and Donna DeLory, and most CD's by John Adorney, especially *Beckoning*, featuring Daya.

Consider the options of having a set playlist or CD that you use for your sessions versus switching your musical environment with various songs or even an advertisement-free Pandora account. Both can work well. I prefer the few sounds that work well for me. This way, when I hear the music starting, I am given a sub-conscious nudge to go deeper and prepare for the work ahead. It is another way for me to step myself deeper into the experience.

Lighting is another area to consider. As I turn lights down low and close my curtains so that only soft light illumines the room, I pace through the familiar steps, again nudging myself onto a well-woven path within of deepening.

Have extra cozy blankets available as many people feel chilly, especially on their feet, when lying down. Blankets also give a feeling of privacy, safety, and snuggling rather than lying vulnerable on a table with eyes closed. For many people this takes a lot of courage.

Ask if your client would like to turn over on their stomachs, or if they prefer a side position. Although the most common position is having a client lay on their back, energy work can be done from any position. The energy goes where it needs to, so the less a person is moved during a session, the deeper they may release to allow healing to occur.

## Guided Visualization

Starting with a gentle guided meditation is a good way to start transitioning from the first to second phase which allows you to help settle someone onto the table and transition to a quiet, deeper, more meditative space. This transition allows the both of you to step through a multidimensional doorway into the healing and energy realm. This is as much for you as it is for the client.

Practice a few guided visualizations until you feel comfortable with the visual setting and the feeling of stepping through the portal. There are many good visualizations and Book 3 of the *Tools for Lightworkers Series* offers a number of them. I like to start with our breath — it is an effortless and endless swing which, when we bring in a moment of conscious awareness, allows us to relax, release, trust, and deepen, all within the space of, well, a breath.

A word about modulating your voice. When transitioning from normal conversation to a guided visualization our voices usually modulate from common patterns to a softer, gentler tone of voice. You are stepping yourself and your client through a portal into a safe, sacred space for healing and, perhaps, a place where higher communications occur for both of you.

There is a sweet spot between the one-note voice register where everything you say is almost hypnotically spoken and our normal inflections of high's and low's. When people think of giving a guided visualization they most times choose this monotone, less reflective, disembodied voice. And that type of patterning may help people relax and even go to sleep.

Another recommendation is to find the moving space between the two. I walk and talk the visualization, moving my hands and body to the respective parts on the client. For example, if I speak about roots coming out of the soles of their feet, I move to the foot of the table, and in the air above their feet I motion the 'roots' coming out of their soles and going down to the earth.

I also speak with a cadence that is soothing, and yet is story-telling, or portal-crossing, not monotone or hypnotic. Try the variations for yourself. Find a comfortable way of helping yourself and your client leave 3D. Ask for feedback or tape yourself and listen with compassion and clarity to your own voice.

Below is a standard guided visualization that I use:

## *Conscious Human Tree Guided Visualization*

*We begin by taking 3 conscious breaths. Observe how good it feels to take in air. It fills us up easily, effortlessly, completely. We don't need to gulp down more air than we need. Just the right amount. We don't need to force or release more air out of our lungs. Just the right amount comes in. Just the right amount goes out. Like a wave. We relax and feel safe in this embrace.*

*Follow your next breath down your body, down your torso, down your legs, and out the soles of your feet. Follow the thread down, as far deep into the Earth that feels comfortable for you. Past the foundation layers you are standing on. Through the soil and water table levels. Down as deep as the core of the Earth if you like. Anchor in where you feel safe.*

*Now breathe up from your roots, from the Earth. Bring the beautiful colors of the Earth up through your feet, up your legs, up your torso, up and out the top of your head like a cascading waterfall of light. Breathe as Earth colors wash through you, bringing rejuvenation, balance, healing, and joy. Bring up the Earth colors – blues and greens, purple, pink, and yellows, oranges, gold, silver, all the wonderful Earth colors come up your torso. They bring the rejuvenating, refreshing Earth energies to every cell and every organ in your body.*

*With your next breath open the top of your head, your crown chakra. Vision your branches and leaves growing up. They ascend upwards and open their canopy outside the Earth, like an umbrella. Breathe in swirling solar colors, down through your branches, down through your head, down your torso, down your roots and into the Earth. These solar and heavenly colors bring pastel colors, pearlescent and iridescent colors, all swirling down through your crown chakra, through your body and into the Earth.*

*The colors carry information and are coded and decoded by the magnetics in your DNA and enter the Earth's magnetics through you, bringing your unique tone into the Earth. Now breathe up again from the Earth, your roots, bringing Earth's magnetic codes through your DNA magnetics, up your crown and into the universe, sounding your unique I AM tone.*

*And here we stand as Conscious Trees.*

*Spanning heaven and earth.*

*Finite and infinite.*

*Mortality and immortality.*

*I call upon the Creator and the Forces of Love and Light.*

*I call upon my Soul, my Highest Self, my direct I AM Lineage to be present with me today.*

*(continue with Prayer of Intent)*

## Conscious Human Tree

On this page is an illustration of a Conscious Human Tree by Mariana Ruzsek. I often visualize this image as I guide client's feet into the earth and branches into the sky.

Write a sample Guided Visualization for a healing session below.

_____

_____

_____

_____

_____

_____

_____

_____

_____

_____

_____

_____

_____

_____

_____

_____

_____

## Prayer of Intent

If you choose, say a verbal Prayer of Intent. If you prefer, it may be silent. Regardless of the delivery, set an intent for the session. And ask your client to give permission for the intent. This is where and when the healing doorway opens.

If you are comfortable (and you will become more so with practice), then listening verbally to the Intent is important for the client to open up and allow for the healing. We do not 'do' anything for them. We prepare and open a healing space which their Higher Selves can step into and claim.

I normally ask if there is anything physically going on with them. Then ask if there is any particular intent they have for the session. It is important for a client to understand exactly what they are asking for, because they just might get it! And, it's important that we don't hold an agenda for them that they are not intending.

With clarity of getting specific information, I will repeat what I heard and then mention that I might broaden it. I ask the client if my words sound right and is this what she is intending? With their approval, I start the Prayer of Intent. I often expand the intent because many times the healing comes with a larger opening. For example, perhaps their left knee hurts. I include their words and I might include "balance and moving forward on all levels in their precious life". It sounds and feels more poetic, sacred, and life affirming rather than intend for someone to have a pain-free left knee.

When there is no specific information coming from a client ("Nothing really, just a session") then I take a moment to check in with Higher Guidance and mention a few possibilities. For example, "....for the intent to feel clear, energized, and in radiant health, walking confidently and surely on his highest destiny path". I ask them if that sounds good or if they would like to change or add anything.

This type of back-and-forth is invaluable in getting the client to set clear intent for the healing, and to open to the process to get their healing.

One last thing to mention is that I 'reach out' when I am adding the specifics and the broadening information, and I am already in an altered state. You might start feeling a little woozy, but you will get used to the feeling. You might get a sense of Guides and Loved Ones coming right in, or you might get an immediate insight into the client's condition. Alternately, you might feel nothing at all, which is also common. Make your best effort to enjoy building and maintaining this sacred healing space, stay out of it as much as you can, and know this is for you as well as for them!

It's wonderful and very empowering to invest time writing your basic Prayer of Intent. It may grow, evolve or change completely, but having a standard opening is a portal for you. It also signals to your Guides that you are ready for the healing work to start. There is space for you to write a basic Prayer of Intent at the end of this section.

Consider you are hosting a party and sending out invitations. There are 4 basic parts to the Prayer of Intent:

1. The invoking or calling in. Begin with an invitation. Who are you calling upon? What are you calling upon? Angels, God, Healing Masters?

_____

_____

_____

A further extension of this invitation is to then call upon the Soul, the Highest Self of the client, and their entourage as well.

_____

_____

_____

2. The intent. What are you and the client intending?

_____

_____

_____

3. Protections and conditions

_____

_____

_____

4. The ending

_____

_____

_____

Following is my beloved Prayer of Intent. More detailed information is available in Book 3 of the Tools for Lightworkers Series, *Prayers of Intent and Guided Visualizations*.

## Sample Prayer of Intent for Healing Session

I call upon the Creator and the Forces of Love and Light. I call upon Jesus, Mary, and the Tower of Strength energies. I call upon the Buddha and Quan Yin, the Goddess of Mercy and Compassion, and the Bodhisattvas through the ages.

I call upon the Angels and Archangels to be present here for this healing, especially upon Michael, Raphael, and (whoever else might be 'present').

I call upon (client's name) to be present here for this healing. I call upon her Soul, her Highest and Greatest Self, her direct I AM lineage. I call upon the Masters, Teachers, and Loved Ones of the Light to be present here for (name),

and for her intent of (specific healing) and (expand to larger arc).

I affirm that we are in protected and safe space (put Cho Ku Rei's in corners again) and that everything that happens here is the Highest and Greatest Good for All.

And So Be It.

Write a sample Prayer of Intent you can use for a healing session below.

_____

_____

_____

_____

_____

_____

_____

_____

_____

_____

_____

_____

_____

_____

_____

_____

## Singing, Chanting, Sound Healing …. or Silence

After the Prayer of Intent, I might be silent as I conduct the session.

Or, most times I feel guided to sing. If you are trained in Karuna Reiki Master, Language of Light Healing Master or Living Fractals of Light Healer (levels 3 – 5 in Lightworker Apprenticeship) then you are trained in using your personal instrument, your voice, as a powerful sound healing technique.

There are many types of sound healing techniques including crystal bowls, Tibetan bowls, tuning forks, drumming, chanting, bells, biaural beats, solfeggio, isochronic tones, nature sounds, sacred songs, and more. Sound waves permeate through all of our subtle bodies as well as our physical cells, organs and systems.

Sound and light are both magnificent healing mediums. It's wonderful to envision healing chambers of the future where sound, light and crystals are used to regenerate and heal rather than endure labs, surgeries, and hospital stays.

Again, use your personal guidance, passion, and discernment in pursuing sound healing methods. In this Apprenticeship I teach sound healing through our own instrument, our voice, in the three advanced healing methods listed above.

If you wish to bring your voice and sound healing to a session, unless you are a trained singer, you might encounter some hesitation and self-judgment. Practice to go beyond these limitations! There is tremendous power and joy in singing a healing. The vibrations well up from inside you and permeate through you and through the client into the healing space where intricate patterns shift and integrate into healing wholeness.

If you are trained in the advanced sound healing methods, sing the symbols into the session. I begin singing in my Angelic name and a Soul name for the client. I then start with *Zonar*, the energy bath, and fill the sound stage with symbols that are guided to come through. The symbol, the notes and octaves, and the repetitive phases and phrases are all guided uniquely for that healing. You must practice to allow for and to trust this synchronicity!

You can sing the symbols and prayers sub-vocally which is a good start, and many times is as effective as singing out loud. Sometimes clients are surprised by your singing and that might inhibit you as well. There are no hard and fast rules, follow your guidance, trust yourself, and, maybe, push yourself a little.

# We are Conductors, Conducting

I often liken what we do in a session to conductors. We are the ones in human form, directing a magnificent orchestra of healers, guides and the client's Higher Self. We are also conducting a micro orchestra of cells, organs, and DNA properties.

Have fun dancing and singing and conducting your way through this majestic symphony of light, love and healing energies!

## Keeping focus during the session

Each healing session is unique. It is sometimes easy to stay with the energies, tracking pain, heat, cold, or sensation through the client's field. Other times we get messages through our higher sense orders. We might 'see' on an inner screen what is happening in the field. We might 'hear' information. We might 'sense' what to do next, where to put our hands next. In the midst of this multidimensional energy and information, there is no problem that we might be distracted or not engaged.

However, there are times when, for a number of reasons, nothing seems to be happening that you can perceive. You get no sense impressions, no 'messages', your mind wanders, or your body is impatient.

In those times, first, it is important to realize that the intent is for the Highest and Greatest Good and the energy is going where it needs to go. You are a conductor, not a generator.

The client might be (and often is) having a very different experience than you are. It happens frequently that you might be experiencing so much (warmth, messages, pain) and the client feels nothing. Conversely, you might be beating yourself up in your inability to focus, and your client is having the most wondrous, exalted experience. So, don't judge!

Sometimes the client is present on the table, but is frightened or closed to feeling anything. They might be guarded or boundaried and you might be engaged with their closed field. With Highest and Greatest Good in mind, you could mention you are checking their feet to see how grounded they are, and ask are they doing a lot of physical activities. Sometimes, this checking-in on something fairly innocuous helps to open things up.

Nevertheless, if you wish to feel more engaged, consider a few options.

> First, ask for help in being more focused and in feeling more of the energy flow happening
>
> Second, do Cho Ku Rei (power symbol!)
>
> Third, move to a different location on the body. Or, if you are moving too much, settle down in one area
>
> Fourth, put your tongue to the roof of your mouth (violet breath) and breathe
>
> Fifth, ask for one symbol or one message to share with your client
>
> Finally, relax, enjoy the music, and trust the process

## Touch and privacy

A final mention about touch. Be pristine. You may always work above the body. Allow for personal privacy. Be aware of how close your face is to theirs, how closely your breath flows near them. Be aware of your arms on their hair, or on their nose. Offer an eye pillow for their comfort and privacy. Have a light touch.

# Sharing Guided Information

For Apprentice energy work practices and circles, it is appropriate to share and even be encouraged to share intuitive insights. It is an art and a matter of integrity, compassion, and sparkling clarity to share information which we feel is guided.

With clients, it is a complex topic.

Reiki is traditionally practiced in silence and intuitive information is not shared. For publicly practiced Reiki sessions, silence is the norm.

What is the basis of the information we may receive for a client? It is important to walk very carefully with your guidance on this issue. On the one hand, we, as vibrational interpreters, are tuning in to the broadcasts from the client and from Beings of Love and Light. It is our responsibility to discern if the information is

> Logical: (it's hot out, client said she loves treats, an ice cream cone popped in my head)
>
> imaginative: (an ice cream cone popped in my head - who knows why? Maybe they should be more like a child)
>
> borderline logical/imaginative: (same storyline, but you work to find the message)
>
> intuitive: (an ice cream cone popped in my mind – I am getting a strong message about being more playful, and experiencing delight in the everyday joys in your life)
>
> guided/channeled: (same storyline, but you can see client as a child eating, or in a past life and everything fits together, including a message)

The best I can say is practice opening up your gifts and then begin to discern the differences between the level of the messages. It will feel higher, lighter, more compassionate, more loving as you move from imaginative to guided. The inner voice of each level is different. Many times, the higher the voice, the more merriment and joy the message.

Then, you make a decision whether to share, what to share, and offer your interpretation of what it could mean. Otherwise, why tell a person you saw an ice cream cone. What would that mean to them? If you don't know what the message means, ask within before saying anything. "Please tell me what this image means. What am I to share with this beloved being of love and light?"

You could also ask the client if the vision means anything to them. You might be picking up their stories, memories, or messages from Loved Ones.

Unfortunately, I have witnessed energy workers share confusing information, or even negative information. This is especially harmful when the person is on the table, under a light trance state, and therefore very vulnerable to a healer's suggestions. To 'share' in this manner seems to be irresponsible and harmful. If you tell a friend over coffee and donuts to leave her husband, she might listen or not. If you tell a client that you were guided by XXXX to tell her to leave her husband, you have taken some of her free will. She 'hears' you on a compromised level. And you are working out of integrity.

Be clear in your intent to do energy work. If you want to be a star – perhaps take up theater. It's less risky. If your intent is to be of service, to be an energy healer, and to be a Lightworker, then ask for compassion, clarity, humility and for Beings of Love and Light to guide and teach you.

## *Be humble in the face of Infinity!*

# Section 18

## Phase 3: Clearing, Integrating and Ending a Healing Session

Ending the session can be done in a number of ways. Because the client can be in a deep state, or even sleeping, it is important to take time and sensitively bring the client back to full consciousness.

Various ways to let the client know the session is over includes touching their feet to give a nonverbal cue that the session is over, touching their arm and mentioning in a soft voice that the session is over and to take their time getting up.

You might also consider lowering the music, opening the curtains or putting a soft light on. The traditional phrase of ending a session is stating, "I seal this healing in with Divine love and wisdom", and drawing a Cho Ku Rei on the client's solar plexus.

Most sessions, I end by singing and motioning in a Song of Blessing for the client. I thank the guides and energies for being present before sealing in the healing. I touch their arm lightly and say, "Welcome back" or something similar. There are a lot of loving feelings at the moment of return!

## Integrate the Client

The client has been on the table for close to an hour in a deep state, so they may need a few minutes to sit up and move around. Be sure to offer them help off the table and encourage them to drink water.

I usually reserve time at the end to share some information I might have gotten for them. Especially with Spectrum Energetics, there are visualizations for different chakras which are offered as fun 'homework' assignments. I write down the information or pictures for them to take home and to reflect upon.

Reminders for clients are to hydrate, eat, take time to relax during the remainder of the day, and reflect upon the session including any memories or information they may have gotten.

Be sure they are not 'woozy' before they leave. Also, encourage them to contact you with any questions they might have and to give you feedback in a few days or a week or two. Those who are new to energy work might need time to realize the subtle movements and changes associated with this type of work.

## Clear Your Environment

After the session is over, consider smudging or diffusing oils and put Cho Ku Rei in the four corners of the room. You will be surprised how heavy and dense the air might feel in your space after a healing session. Although it is a good entrée into multidimensional space and intuitive work, best to clear it completely for a fresh start and to ground your space.

Change your music and lighting. Clear and change your linens. Tidy up.

Rocks and plants are good to have in your sacred area to help ground. A client once brought me a 'hearth stone' to balance my space as it is very ethereally focused. Crystals can serve this purpose too, but I mainly use crystals for intuitive guidance and rocks for grounding. Find favorite ones to stay with you – I have rock friends, shells, feathers, sand, and an deer antler stub all which have been with me for decades.

## Clear and Honor Yourself and the Session

I ground myself by getting fresh air, drinking water or tea, eating, and resting, if I can. Wash your hands which will help break contact.

Spend time within yourself, reflecting upon the session and giving thanks for this sacred work we are so privileged and honored to do. Jot down notes from your session. Put their name or their intent under a candle or Reiki Grid so that you can continue to send to their healing and empowerment during the next few days and weeks.

Try not to run into the next activity, jump online, or return phone calls or emails. You have just navigated through dimensions. Welcome yourself back gently!

# Summary of Conducting a Healing Session

## Phase 1:  Preparation

✓ Prepare yourself by wearing sacred clothes, colors, jewelry; sing your Angelic name, symbols, chants

✓ Reiki yourself and align chakras; meditate to align with your Center

✓ Use oils, open Angel Wings; affirmations of mastery

✓ <u>YOU are the resonance</u>!

✓ Prepare the space by smudging;  play inspirational music

✓ Put Reiki symbols in room and Cho Ku Rei in corners

✓ YOU are there to facilitate the healing!

✓ Prepare the client by asking questions, getting their intent

## Phase 2:  Conducting the Session

✓ Grounding client to earth, open to heavens;

✓ Use crystals or oils

✓ Prayer of Intent; Ask for permission for healing

✓ Highest and Greatest Good – no agenda

✓ Ask for Vibrational Records to access if you wish to access past life

✓ YOU are the One opening the multidimensional portal to their Higher Self and healing

## Phase 3:  Clearing Afterwards

✓ Bring client back to 3D

✓ Offer them water, allow time for them to ground

✓ Share impressions if guided to

✓ Encourage them to drink water, rest and give feedback

✓ Smudge, Cho Ku Rei in ceiling corners

✓ Wash hands to clear energy; go outdoors; drink water

✓ Clear table & linens; take notes

✓ Give thanks

✓ Water!

# *Summary of Chapter 6*

## Healing Sessions

What are additional ways you prepare for a session?

_____

_____

_____

_____

_____

_____

_____

_____

_____

_____

_____

_____

_____

_____

What are additional ways you enjoy conducting a session?

_____

_____

_____

_____

_____

_____

_____

_____

_____

_____

_____

_____

_____

_____

_____

_____

_____

_____

What are additional ways you integrate and clear after a session?

_____

_____

_____

_____

_____

_____

_____

_____

_____

_____

_____

_____

_____

_____

_____

_____

*We span heaven and earth, finite and infinite,*
*mortality and immortality!*

# Part 3

# Holding a Mandalic Consciousness: Reflections and Feedback

# Introduction

# A Fish in the Ocean, We Swim in Sacred Patterns

In Part 3, we are offered worksheets to reflect and document various aspects of our Lightworker Orientation and Training. We can more easily see the overall image of our training, and, we look for patterns.

There are many ways in which aspects of our lives are interconnected. Physicists might call this type of interconnectedness 'entanglement'. Mandalas, consciousness, and patterns (fractals) all play a part in our growth and our intent to serve as Lightworkers, or Lighthouses, shining light in these times.

## Mandalas, Fractals and Consciousness

Mandala means 'sacred circle' and there are examples of mandalas used as forms of ancient artwork by Native Americans, Buddhists, Hindus, Celts and other indigenous tribes. They are used traditionally for healing, meditation, mindfulness, and developing spiritual insight. We see the whole and the parts.

Carl Jung wrote about mandalas when he described coming into a conscious realization of our wholeness while merging opposites within us. In a mandala, one can move through personal issues, even opposite characteristics, in a sacred way. Mandalas help us to direct our attention inward towards wholeness, harmony, and truth.

'Consciousness' has had a history of over 100 years in American psychology of being heretical, unnecessary, unknowable, and therefore not of any researchable purpose in motivation, learning, or moving the self forward. With the pioneering work of transpersonalists and noetic scientists, consciousness is finally beginning to make its way into mainstream psychology. The definition of consciousness is the upper level of mental states, being awake, perceiving the whole. Here, we use consciousness to mean the totality of our vibrational signature.

Fractals are geometric repeating patterns. They have been studied for hundreds of years, but Mandlebrot coined the term 'fractal' in 1975 and set off a storm of recognition and remembrance. Nature is a fractal mandala – consider a leaf, a storm, a cell, a galaxy, a snowflake. Nature is a fractal mandala. Our lives hold fractals – repeating patterns. And we gather them into a sacred whole – a mandala of our consciousness.

A 'mandalic consciousness' is one in which we see the whole within the parts. May you see the whole within your parts!

# Chapter 7

# Discerning

# Sacred

# Patterns

# Discerning Sacred Patterns

Chapter 7 offers us 7 lenses to discern patterns that might repeat in our lives, and especially through our energy trainings. These different fractal images of our work allow us to more clearly step into our Lightworker identity.

Do you judge yourself critically? Are you afraid 'all this' might not be true? What are the hidden core beliefs that come up for release? Do you wish you were more intuitive? Do you dearly want to do this work but are afraid of ...? These inner patterns form the sacred art in our lives, our mandalas of consciousness.

In this chapter we journal through the year in a number of ways. We do this for personal sessions, group meetings, partnering with others in our Apprentice group to send Reiki and to practice intuitive arts. We also send as Lightworkers every month to personal, community and global issues that are important to us. Finally, we cast a glimpse at a larger, more expansive celestial environment.

Through our reflections we uncover the fractals of our mandalic consciousness. Perhaps we might choose to shift some of the patterns. Perhaps we wish to acknowledge and honor the patterns.

## Teleidoscopic and Kaleidoscopic Visions

A teleidoscope has a lens with an open view so that it can form patterns outside the tool itself whereas a kaleidoscope offers images from items already installed within the tube. When you hold a kaleidoscope you see what is imprinted within. When you hold a teleidoscope, you turn your attention outward and see the patterns created by whatever you turn your attention to outwardly.

Here we turn our attention and focus on feedback and reflections of our work together to discern the underlying sacred patterns in our lives and our Light work.

# Chapter 7 Overview

Seven worksheets are offered for your pleasure!

These 7 worksheets cover:

| | | |
|---|---|---|
| Section 19: | Personal session notes: 12 months | |
| | (monthly private sessions with me) | |
| Section 20: | Apprentice group meetings: 12 months | |
| | (monthly group meetings) | |
| Section 21: | Client/healing sessions: 30 sessions | |
| | (recommended sessions for feedback from me) | |
| Section 22: | Lightworkers, Lighting Up! | |
| | (monthly focal points after Reiki Circle) | |
| Section 23: | Partnering:  Send and Receive  Reiki | |
| | (3 worksheets for feedback and reflection) | |
| Section 24: | Partnering on intuition and higher gifts | |
| | (3 worksheets for feedback and reflection) | |
| Section 25: | Celestial broadcasts | |
| | (seasonal, moon and stellar reflections) | |

Each of these worksheets serve as a feedback loop for you, a referral and inspiration source, and as valuable fractal patterning information for our holistic or Mandalic personal consciousness.

Feel free to bring questions or comments on these worksheets during our monthly meetings or your personal session.

EnJoy!

# Section 19

## Reflections on Personal Sessions

Once a month we meet for a personal session. Looking within is our map and our compass. Trust that the issues you bring, the sacred details of your daily life – all are important fractal parts of our mandala of wholeness. We live in an interconnected field. The challenges you face can benefit others. Perhaps you will one day be able to shine a light on an area that you have dedicated time to understanding and clearing. Perhaps you will 'just' vibrate the solution and the clarity out into the world as the Lightworker you are without ever saying a word to anyone. And, because we work multidimensionally, you are also beaming or shining your light vibration through time as well.

Lightworker, light up! Release the feeling of personal drama and embrace the understanding that we all share the same stories. It is not personal as much as it is universal. And that knowledge allows us to dig deep within, shine light, and set healings and empowerments in place.

You might get information on your Inner Child, inner landscapes, soul-based perspectives on your current life experiences. We work with your Guides, your Higher Self and Beings of Love and Light to bring you the highest understandings, healings and gifts.

It is wonderful to take a soul perspective on our journey. Go higher than walking through our personal terrain. Take a helicopter for a wider perspective. Can't see enough of the pattern and gift? Take a jet plane/ 35,000 mile perspective. If you still want to go higher, take a space shuttle view. Everything looks perfect, awe-inspiring, and beloved from that on- high view.

After each session, consider writing the information that is shared with you, and your reflections afterwards. At the end, read through your personal sessions and have fun summarizing the wisdom, changes, and clarity you have encountered.

I am always honored to witness your sacred stories. And, most times, I have walked some of this journey myself, or you would not be here with me.

*In Lach'ech*
*(Mayan, "I am another yourself")*

1.    Personal Session Date:

Guided Information

_____

_____

_____

_____

_____

"Homework"

_____

_____

_____

_____

_____

Reflections

_____

_____

_____

_____

_____

2.    Personal Session Date:

Guided Information

_____

_____

_____

_____

_____

"Homework"

_____

_____

_____

_____

_____

Reflections

_____

_____

_____

_____

_____

3.     Personal Session Date:

Guided Information

_____

_____

_____

_____

_____

_____

"Homework"

_____

_____

_____

_____

_____

Reflections

_____

_____

_____

_____

_____

4.    Personal Session Date:

Guided Information

_____

_____

_____

_____

_____

_____

"Homework"

_____

_____

_____

_____

_____

Reflections

_____

_____

_____

_____

_____

5.   Personal Session Date:

Guided Information

_____

_____

_____

_____

_____

"Homework"

_____

_____

_____

_____

_____

Reflections

_____

_____

_____

_____

_____

6.    Personal Session Date:

Guided Information

_____

_____

_____

_____

_____

"Homework"

_____

_____

_____

_____

_____

Reflections

_____

_____

_____

_____

_____

7.    Personal Session Date:

Guided Information

_____

_____

_____

_____

_____

_____

"Homework"

_____

_____

_____

_____

_____

Reflections

_____

_____

_____

_____

_____

_____

8.    Personal Session Date:

### Guided Information

_____

_____

_____

_____

_____

### "Homework"

_____

_____

_____

_____

_____

### Reflections

_____

_____

_____

_____

_____

9.   Personal Session Date:

### Guided Information

_____

_____

_____

_____

_____

### "Homework"

_____

_____

_____

_____

### Reflections

_____

_____

_____

_____

_____

10.  Personal Session Date:

Guided Information

_____

_____

_____

_____

_____

_____

"Homework"

_____

_____

_____

_____

_____

Reflections

_____

_____

_____

_____

_____

11. Personal Session Date:

## Guided Information

_____

_____

_____

_____

_____

## "Homework"

_____

_____

_____

_____

_____

## Reflections

_____

_____

_____

_____

_____

12.   Personal Session Date:

Guided Information

_____

_____

_____

_____

_____

_____

"Homework"

_____

_____

_____

_____

_____

Reflections

_____

_____

_____

_____

_____

## Summary of Personal Sessions

Were there any recurrent themes of your sessions?

_____

_____

_____

_____

_____

Did you feel movement occur in stuck or unclear areas?

_____

_____

_____

_____

_____

Were there any special moments or messages you received?

_____

_____

_____

_____

_____

Anything else you wish to honor and reflect upon about your personal sessions?

_____

_____

_____

_____

_____

_____

_____

_____

_____

_____

_____

_____

_____

_____

_____

_____

_____

# Section 20

## Reflections on Apprentice Group Meetings

Every month we meet as a group and work our way through the trainings, tools and techniques of energy work and of being a Lightworker.

Every monthly meeting is unique. We work off the basic syllabus for the year, but we also honor when organic or overarching matters take center stage. Trust in the process that we all intend 'Highest and Greatest Good for All'!

Take time each month to capture some of the information for your files.

EnJoy!

1.   Apprentice Group Meeting Date:

Notes

_____

_____

_____

_____

_____

Reflections

_____

_____

_____

_____

_____

Follow-Up

_____

_____

_____

_____

_____

_____

2.    Apprentice Group Meeting Date:

Notes

_____

_____

_____

_____

_____

Reflections

_____

_____

_____

_____

Follow-Up

_____

_____

_____

_____

_____

_____

3.    Apprentice Group Meeting Date:

Notes

_____

_____

_____

_____

_____

Reflections

_____

_____

_____

_____

_____

Follow-Up

_____

_____

_____

_____

_____

_____

4.     Apprentice Group Meeting Date:

Notes

_____

_____

_____

_____

_____

Reflections

_____

_____

_____

_____

Follow-Up

_____

_____

_____

_____

_____

5.    Apprentice Group Meeting Date:

Notes

_____

_____

_____

_____

_____

_____

Reflections

_____

_____

_____

_____

_____

Follow-Up

_____

_____

_____

_____

_____

_____

_____

6.  Apprentice Group Meeting Date:

Notes

_____

_____

_____

_____

_____

Reflections

_____

_____

_____

_____

_____

Follow-Up

_____

_____

_____

_____

_____

7.     Apprentice Group Meeting Date:

Notes

_____

_____

_____

_____

_____

Reflections

_____

_____

_____

_____

Follow-Up

_____

_____

_____

_____

_____

_____

8.  Apprentice Group Meeting Date:

Notes

_____

_____

_____

_____

_____

Reflections

_____

_____

_____

_____

_____

Follow-Up

_____

_____

_____

_____

_____

_____

9.    Apprentice Group Meeting Date:

Notes

_____

_____

_____

_____

_____

_____

Reflections

_____

_____

_____

_____

_____

Follow-Up

_____

_____

_____

_____

_____

_____

_____

10. Apprentice Group Meeting Date:

Notes

_____

_____

_____

_____

_____

Reflections

_____

_____

_____

_____

_____

Follow-Up

_____

_____

_____

_____

_____

11. Apprentice Group Meeting Date:

Notes

_____

_____

_____

_____

_____

Reflections

_____

_____

_____

_____

_____

Follow-Up

_____

_____

_____

_____

_____

_____

12.    Apprentice Group Meeting Date:

Notes

_____

_____

_____

_____

_____

Reflections

_____

_____

_____

_____

_____

Follow-Up

_____

_____

_____

_____

_____

_____

# Summary of Apprentice Group Meetings

Reflect on your overall experience in our group Apprentice meetings. Did you feel comfortable expressing the Light you are? Are you comfortable with group exchanges? Can you see yourself running groups on Lightwork?

_____

_____

_____

_____

_____

_____

_____

_____

Anything else you wish to honor and reflect upon about our group sessions?

_____

_____

_____

_____

_____

_____

_____

# Section 21

## 30 Client/Healing Sessions

As part of our Arise Apprenticeship training, you are encouraged to complete and document 30 energy healing sessions.

You may include healings on yourself, friends, family, animal companions and distance sending.

Many can be short documentations, but consider investing the time and energy to thoroughly document at least 6 sessions more completely for consultation with me during one of your monthly sessions.

The following 24 pages are offered for your short documentations.

The final 6 page sets are for your longer healing reflections and feedback.

EnJOY this precious work!

## Client Session Notes

Date Session #1: _____

Client Self / Distance session:

_____

Focus for Session:

_____

_____

_____

_____

_____

_____

Quick Notes:

_____

_____

_____

_____

_____

_____

_____

_____

## Client Session Notes

Date Session #2: _____

Client Self / Distance session:

_____

Focus for Session:

_____

_____

_____

_____

_____

_____

Quick Notes:

_____

_____

_____

_____

_____

_____

_____

_____

## Client Session Notes

Date Session #3: _____

Client Self / Distance session:

_____

Focus for Session:

_____

_____

_____

_____

_____

_____

Quick Notes:

_____

_____

_____

_____

_____

_____

_____

_____

## Client Session Notes

Date Session #4: _____

Client Self / Distance session:

_____

Focus for Session:

_____

_____

_____

_____

_____

_____

Quick Notes:

_____

_____

_____

_____

_____

_____

_____

_____

## Client Session Notes

Date Session #5: _____

Client Self / Distance session:

_____

Focus for Session:

_____

_____

_____

_____

_____

_____

Quick Notes:

_____

_____

_____

_____

_____

_____

_____

_____

## Client Session Notes

Date Session #6: _____

Client Self / Distance session:

_____

Focus for Session:

_____

_____

_____

_____

_____

_____

Quick Notes:

_____

_____

_____

_____

_____

_____

_____

_____

## Client Session Notes

Date Session #7: _____

Client Self / Distance session:

_____

Focus for Session:

_____

_____

_____

_____

_____

_____

Quick Notes:

_____

_____

_____

_____

_____

_____

_____

_____

## Client Session Notes

Date Session #8: _____

Client Self / Distance session:

_____

Focus for Session:

_____

_____

_____

_____

_____

_____

Quick Notes:

_____

_____

_____

_____

_____

_____

_____

_____

Client Session Notes

Date Session #9: _____

Client Self / Distance session:

_____

Focus for Session:

_____

_____

_____

_____

_____

_____

Quick Notes:

_____

_____

_____

_____

_____

_____

_____

_____

## Client Session Notes

Date Session #10: _____

Client Self / Distance session:

_____

Focus for Session:

_____

_____

_____

_____

_____

_____

Quick Notes:

_____

_____

_____

_____

_____

_____

_____

_____

## Client Session Notes

Date Session #11: _____

Client Self / Distance session:

_____

Focus for Session:

_____

_____

_____

_____

_____

_____

Quick Notes:

_____

_____

_____

_____

_____

_____

_____

_____

## Client Session Notes

Date Session #12: _____

Client Self / Distance session:

_____

Focus for Session:

_____

_____

_____

_____

_____

_____

Quick Notes:

_____

_____

_____

_____

_____

_____

_____

_____

## Client Session Notes

Date Session #13: _____

Client Self / Distance session:

_____

Focus for Session:

_____

_____

_____

_____

_____

_____

Quick Notes:

_____

_____

_____

_____

_____

_____

_____

_____

## Client Session Notes

Date Session #14: _____

Client Self / Distance session:

_____

Focus for Session:

_____

_____

_____

_____

_____

_____

Quick Notes:

_____

_____

_____

_____

_____

_____

_____

_____

## Client Session Notes

Date Session #15: _____

Client Self / Distance session:

_____

Focus for Session:

_____

_____

_____

_____

_____

_____

Quick Notes:

_____

_____

_____

_____

_____

_____

_____

_____

## Client Session Notes

Date Session #16: _____

Client Self / Distance session:

_____

Focus for Session:

_____

_____

_____

_____

_____

_____

Quick Notes:

_____

_____

_____

_____

_____

_____

_____

_____

Client Session Notes

Date Session #17: _____

Client Self / Distance session:

_____

Focus for Session:

_____

_____

_____

_____

_____

_____

Quick Notes:

_____

_____

_____

_____

_____

_____

_____

_____

## Client Session Notes

Date Session #18: _____

Client Self / Distance session:

_____

Focus for Session:

_____

_____

_____

_____

_____

_____

Quick Notes:

_____

_____

_____

_____

_____

_____

_____

_____

## Client Session Notes

Date Session #19: _____

Client Self / Distance session:

_____

Focus for Session:

_____

_____

_____

_____

_____

_____

Quick Notes:

_____

_____

_____

_____

_____

_____

_____

_____

## Client Session Notes

Date Session #20: _____

Client Self / Distance session:

_____

Focus for Session:

_____

_____

_____

_____

_____

_____

Quick Notes:

_____

_____

_____

_____

_____

_____

_____

_____

## Client Session Notes

Date Session #21: _____

Client Self / Distance session:

_____

Focus for Session:

_____

_____

_____

_____

_____

_____

Quick Notes:

_____

_____

_____

_____

_____

_____

_____

_____

Client Session Notes

Date Session #22: _____

Client Self / Distance session:

_____

Focus for Session:

_____

_____

_____

_____

_____

_____

Quick Notes:

_____

_____

_____

_____

_____

_____

_____

_____

Client Session Notes

Date Session #23: _____

Client Self / Distance session:

_____

Focus for Session:

_____

_____

_____

_____

_____

_____

Quick Notes:

_____

_____

_____

_____

_____

_____

_____

_____

Client Session Notes

Date Session #24: _____

Client Self / Distance session:

_____

Focus for Session:

_____

_____

_____

_____

_____

_____

Quick Notes:

_____

_____

_____

_____

_____

_____

_____

_____

## More Detailed Sessions!

Date Session #25:_____

Client /Self / Distance session:

_____

Focus for Session:

_____

_____

_____

Reflections from you - how the energy manifested:

_____

_____

_____

_____

Feedback from Client:

_____

_____

_____

_____

_____

_____

Challenges (if any):

_____

_____

_____

_____

_____

_____

Gifts:

_____

_____

_____

_____

_____

Follow-up:

_____

_____

_____

_____

_____

_____

## More Detailed Sessions!

Date Session #26: _____

Client /Self / Distance session:

_____

Focus for Session:

_____

_____

_____

_____

Reflections from you - how the energy manifested:

_____

_____

_____

_____

_____

Feedback from Client:

_____

_____

_____

_____

_____

_____

Challenges (if any):

_____

_____

_____

_____

_____

Gifts:

_____

_____

_____

_____

_____

Follow-up:

_____

_____

_____

_____

_____

More Detailed Sessions!

Date Session #27:_____

Client /Self / Distance session:

_____

Focus for Session:

_____

_____

_____

_____

Reflections from you - how the energy manifested:

_____

_____

_____

_____

_____

_____

Feedback from Client:

_____

_____

_____

_____

_____

_____

Challenges (if any):

_____

_____

_____

_____

_____

_____

Gifts:

_____

_____

_____

_____

_____

Follow-up:

_____

_____

_____

_____

_____

_____

## More Detailed Sessions!

Date Session #28:_____

Client /Self / Distance session:

_____

Focus for Session:

_____

_____

_____

_____

Reflections from you - how the energy manifested:

_____

_____

_____

_____

_____

Feedback from Client:

_____

_____

_____

_____

_____

Challenges (if any):

_____

_____

_____

_____

_____

_____

Gifts:

_____

_____

_____

_____

_____

Follow-up:

_____

_____

_____

_____

_____

## More Detailed Sessions!

Date Session #29:_____

Client /Self / Distance session:

_____

Focus for Session:

_____

_____

_____

_____

Reflections from you - how the energy manifested:

_____

_____

_____

_____

_____

_____

Feedback from Client:

_____

_____

_____

_____

_____

_____

Challenges (if any):

_____

_____

_____

_____

_____

_____

Gifts:

_____

_____

_____

_____

_____

Follow-up:

_____

_____

_____

_____

_____

_____

## More Detailed Sessions!

Date Session #30:_____

Client /Self / Distance session:

_____

Focus for Session:

_____

_____

_____

_____

Reflections from you - how the energy manifested:

_____

_____

_____

_____

_____

_____

Feedback from Client:

_____

_____

_____

_____

_____

_____

Challenges (if any):

_____

_____

_____

_____

_____

_____

Gifts:

_____

_____

_____

_____

_____

_____

Follow-up:

_____

_____

_____

_____

_____

_____

# Summary Reflections on Client/Healing Sessions

Here is a moment to review your past 30 session.

     How many were:

Self            _____

Family        _____

Friends       _____

Animal Companions    _____

Distance Sending      _____

What did you feel went well during your sessions? Consider set-up, ambience, your ease and comfort, client feedback, ending session, follow-up).

_____

_____

_____

_____

_____

_____

_____

_____

_____

_____

_____

_____

Is there anything you wish to implement going forward?

_____

_____

_____

_____

_____

_____

_____

_____

_____

_____

_____

_____

_____

_____

_____

*You are recognized and honored for this dedicated service, Lightworker!*

# Section 22

## Embracing Lightwork!

### Visions, Dreams, Prayers, Distance Sending, Guided Information

On our unique Earth walk, we are drawn to situations that call to us, either from our own past experiences with those areas, or because our hearts are drawn, like magnets, to the site. Trust the calling.

Shining our light of compassion, empathy, clarity, understanding, tolerance, justice ... there are many frequencies to tune our conscious intent. And, there are so many opportunities to heal, soothe, inspire, uplift, encourage. This is the Bodhisattva path!

We do this many ways including our prayers, dreams, hopes, and visions for a better day. We do this with sending Reiki and light energies out through time and space. And, we also do this by accessing higher, intuitive information through meditation, reflection, inspired readings, community service, and guided dialoguing with higher beings, as in automatic writing.

To capture and embrace our Light work, each month we will focus on three major areas. Keep notes on your sending, and your possible feedback.

1.  Each month, consider a <u>personal situation</u> and offer this situation for all of us to send to. You do not need to share personal information – just basics (relationship, health) is fine!

2.  For our Lightwork community, we will send to everyone's personal or family/friend concerns. It is important to remember we need permission from others to send to them!

3.  For our global community, we will send to whatever issues are important to our community each month.

4.  At the end of the 12 months, review these sending 'contracts' to determine any patterns, passions of yours, and feedback we have gotten from others on our Light work.

For example, you may be living with a sick cat.

If you wish, we all will send to your kitty (personal)

A few others might ask for sending for their home situations (community)

You might also be drawn to the plight of homeless, stray, lab, or feral cats (global).  We can call upon the Feline Angels to help.


*We incarnated for the party.... And here we are!*

Lightwork Month 1: _____

Personal

_____

_____

_____

_____

Lightwork Community

_____

_____

_____

_____

Global

_____

_____

_____

_____

Feedback

_____

_____

_____

_____

Lightwork Month 2: _____

Personal

_____

_____

_____

_____

Lightwork Community

_____

_____

_____

_____

Global

_____

_____

_____

_____

Feedback

_____

_____

_____

_____

Lightwork Month 3: _____

Personal

_____

_____

_____

_____

Lightwork Community

_____

_____

_____

_____

Global

_____

_____

_____

_____

Feedback

_____

_____

_____

_____

Lightwork Month 4: _____

Personal

_____

_____

_____

_____

Lightwork Community

_____

_____

_____

_____

Global

_____

_____

_____

_____

Feedback

_____

_____

_____

_____

Lightwork Month 5: _____

Personal

_____

_____

_____

_____

Lightwork Community

_____

_____

_____

_____

_____

Global

_____

_____

_____

_____

Feedback

_____

_____

_____

_____

Lightwork Month 6: _____

Personal

_____

_____

_____

_____

Lightwork Community

_____

_____

_____

_____

Global

_____

_____

_____

_____

Feedback

_____

_____

_____

_____

Lightwork Month 7: _____

Personal

_____

_____

_____

_____

Lightwork Community

_____

_____

_____

_____

Global

_____

_____

_____

_____

Feedback

_____

_____

_____

_____

Lightwork Month 8: _____

Personal

_____

_____

_____

_____

Lightwork Community

_____

_____

_____

_____

_____

Global

_____

_____

_____

_____

_____

Feedback

_____

_____

_____

_____

Lightwork Month 9: _____

Personal

_____

_____

_____

_____

Lightwork Community

_____

_____

_____

_____

Global

_____

_____

_____

_____

Feedback

_____

_____

_____

_____

Lightwork Month 10: _____

Personal

_____

_____

_____

_____

Lightwork Community

_____

_____

_____

_____

Global

_____

_____

_____

_____

Feedback

_____

_____

_____

_____

Lightwork Month 11: _____

Personal

_____

_____

_____

_____

Lightwork Community

_____

_____

_____

_____

_____

Global

_____

_____

_____

_____

Feedback

_____

_____

_____

_____

Lightwork Month 12: _____

Personal

_____

_____

_____

_____

Lightwork Community

_____

_____

_____

_____

Global

_____

_____

_____

_____

Feedback

_____

_____

_____

_____

# Summary of Lightworkers Lighting Up!

As you review the past months, are there certain areas or patterns that you see for:

Personal:

_____

_____

_____

Our Lightwork Community

_____

_____

_____

Global:

_____

_____

_____

_____

Any patterns of feedback that you discern?

_____

_____

_____

_____

_____

What wisdom and understandings have you gained from your dedicated, daily Lightwork?

_____

_____

_____

_____

_____

_____

_____

_____

_____

_____

_____

_____

_____

_____

_____

# Section 23

## Partnering and Feedback: Send and Receive Reiki

Date: _____

Who are you partnering with to send Reiki?

_____

Issue:

_____

_____

_____

Feedback:

_____

_____

_____

_____

Reflections:

_____

_____

_____

_____

_____

_____

_____

## Partnering to Send Reiki

Date: _____

Who are you partnering with to send Reiki?

_____

Issue:

_____

_____

_____

_____

Feedback:

_____

_____

_____

_____

_____

Reflections:

_____

_____

_____

_____

_____

_____

_____

_____

## Partnering to Send Reiki

Date: _____

Who are you partnering with to send Reiki?

_____

Issue:

_____

_____

_____

_____

Feedback:

_____

_____

_____

_____

Reflections:

_____

_____

_____

_____

_____

_____

_____

_____

# Summary on Sending and Receiving Reiki

How did you like sending Reiki?

_____

_____

_____

_____

_____

Do you feel comfortable sending and receiving Reiki?

_____

_____

_____

_____

_____

_____

Would you like to do more sending Reiki?

_____

_____

_____

_____

_____

_____

What is the difference, if any, between sending and hands-on Reiki?

_____

_____

_____

_____

_____

_____

_____

_____

_____

_____

_____

_____

_____

_____

_____

_____

_____

# Section 24

## Partnering: Intuitive and Higher Gift Orders

Date:_____

Who are you partnering with for intuitive play?

_____

_____

_____

What senses did you use (visual, aural, kinesthetic, empathic, etc.)

_____

_____

_____

Feedback:

_____

_____

_____

Reflections:

_____

_____

_____

_____

_____

Partnering For Intuitive Play

Date:_____

Who are you partnering with for intuitive play?

_____

_____

_____

What senses did you use (visual, aural, kinesthetic, empathic, etc.)

_____

_____

_____

Feedback:

_____

_____

_____

_____

_____

Reflections:

_____

_____

_____

_____

_____

_____

Date:_____

Who are you partnering with for intuitive play?

_____

_____

_____

What senses did you use (visual, aural, kinesthetic, empathic, etc.)

_____

_____

_____

_____

Feedback:

_____

_____

_____

_____

Reflections:

_____

_____

_____

_____

_____

_____

# Summary on Intuitive and Higher Gift Orders

How did you like intuitive play?

_____

_____

_____

_____

What senses did you try?

_____

_____

_____

_____

_____

Do you have a major sense of intuition?

_____

_____

_____

_____

_____

_____

_____

_____

# Section 25

## Celestial Broadcasts

### Spring Equinox

Spring is a time of growth, blossoming newness, and birth.

What would you love to see birth in your life?

_____

_____

_____

_____

_____

_____

_____

_____

What would you love to see birthed in our world?

_____

_____

_____

_____

_____

_____

_____

Together, we broadcast new beginnings, new joys:

_____

_____

_____

_____

_____

_____

_____

_____

_____

_____

_____

_____

_____

_____

_____

_____

_____

_____

## Summer Solstice

Summer is a time of bursting forth in abundance, of bringing to maturity, of family joys and vacations.

What would you love to see grow and mature in your life?

_____

_____

_____

_____

_____

_____

_____

What would you love to see growing and maturing in our world?

_____

_____

_____

_____

_____

_____

_____

_____

Together we broadcast growing and maturing in:

_____

_____

_____

_____

_____

_____

_____

_____

_____

_____

_____

_____

_____

_____

_____

_____

## Autumn Equinox

Autumn is a time of harvesting in all that we have grown, and experiencing swirling changes.

What are you harvesting in your life? What is swirling and chaning?

_____

_____

_____

_____

_____

_____

_____

_____

What are we harvesting in our world? What is swirling and changing?

_____

_____

_____

_____

_____

_____

_____

_____

_____

Together we broadcast harvesting in our growth, and remaining calm in the swirling changing times:

_____

_____

_____

_____

_____

_____

_____

_____

_____

_____

_____

_____

_____

_____

_____

_____

## Winter Solstice

Winter is a time of death and rebirth. It is a time of rest, and deep renewal. It is dreaming and visioning times.

What is dying and rebirthing in your life? What visions are you dreaming?

_____

_____

_____

_____

_____

_____

_____

What is dying and rebirthing in our world? What visions are being dreamed?

_____

_____

_____

_____

_____

_____

_____

_____

_____

Together we broadcast the ever turning, yet ever renewing earth rounds. We broadcast dreams of:

_____

_____

_____

_____

_____

_____

_____

_____

_____

_____

_____

_____

_____

_____

_____

_____

_____

## Moon Cycles

Do you follow moon cycles?  If you do, have you noticed any patterns for yourself or others?

_____

_____

_____

_____

_____

_____

_____

_____

_____

_____

_____

_____

_____

_____

As we follow earth rhythms and pulses, we can honor the more subtle cycles of beginning projects of the new and waxing moon, the blossoming of the full moon, and the diminishing of the waning moon. For those in the mental health, birthing, and law enforcement fields, the influence of the moon is very noticeable.

## Other Celestial Neighbors

Do you follow any eclipses, comets, or planets in the night sky?  If you do, have you noticed any patterns?

_____

_____

_____

_____

_____

_____

_____

_____

_____

_____

_____

_____

*We live in a vibrant celestial environment and are always bombarded by the solar wind, galactic particles, and traveling through parts of space not encountered before. We are soaring in a vortex pattern around our sun.  Our entire solar system is flying at 140 miles a second, or 515,000 miles an hour. The Milky Way has over 200 billion stars and there are billions of galaxies we can see. That's a lot of possible celestial influences. We are vibrational interpreters. Let's claim our solar and galactic heritage!*

# Summary of Chapter 7

## Holding a Mandalic Consciousness:

### Reflections and Feedback

We have covered many types of reflections and feedback from clients and partners. Has this added to your Lightworker identity?

_____

_____

_____

_____

_____

_____

_____

_____

_____

_____

_____

_____

_____

*Calling all Angels!!*

# Part 4

# Lightworker, Light Up!

# *Light Up!*

We have committed ourselves to a Lightworker path. Now what?

The details of our lives, the choices, large and small, the external circumstances, each breath – we are creating and living our lives moment by moment.

Part 4 expands our perspective about what it means to be a Lightworker and gives support for stepping out into the larger community, feeling comfortable and confident in our profession.

# Part 4 Overview

There are three final chapters in Part 4. You will find keys to our journey to help us stay centered and focused on our work, even in the hardest of times. And, although it seems paradoxical, even in the best of times. As we remember who we are and what our focus is, the rest falls into place.

I once had the honor of witnessing and midwifing a wonderful woman who was dying of a rare thyroid cancer. Her name was Sue and she was such an inspiration. I never heard her complain, even with bed sores and diminished mobility. She was grateful for a sliver of avocado, as this was the only thing that could slip down her throat without pain. She was grateful her son came to visit and turn her over on her mattress.

Her only sorrow was that she came to Portland to do Lightwork and she felt there was more to do, so she didn't understand why she was dying. "I know I'm here in Portland for a purpose", she would say.

And, as the end approached and she slipped closer to her transition, I saw very clearly that she did, indeed, travel to Portland to do her Lightwork. She inspired me and everyone who came in contact with her with her gratitude and appreciation for the smallest acts of kindness and relief, and with her willingness to face her transition with so much grace and anticipation.

As I make my way through my daily travails, I often think of Sue. If she could smile and be joyful throughout her painful death, so can we all light up our lives moment by moment, breath by breath.

Chapter 8 allows final reflections on staying balanced and enjoying our work. There are 33 reminders and remembrances in honor of 33 as a Master number reflecting the unity of body/mind/soul, completion, and our DNA complement.

Chapter 9 delves a little deeper into the quantum and multidimensional realm. Enjoy not only some quantum fun, but also archetypes, angelic lineages and expanded chakra meditation.

Chapter 10 is a monthly encouragement to experience mudras and mantras, using our bodies to elevate our consciousness

Chapter 11 (again, a Master number of Illumination) encourages us in broadcasting our unique vibrations by expanding our personal and professional identities. The world needs all Lightworkers to light up!

We end with two prayers. The first is the Shantideva, the Boddhisatva prayer. Boddhisatvas are Beings who have elevated beyond Earth understandings but who choose to stay until every soul is enlightened.   The second is the Peace Prayer of St. Francis. Let us all be instruments of peace!

EnJoy bringing everything together and stepping forward on your Highest Destiny Path!

# Chapter 8

# Consciously Create

# Lightworker

# Identity

# We Look in the True Mirror and See...

Ourselves!

This title reminds of two things. The first is a recollection from childhood, being on a stage in St. Michael's elementary school for a Brownie Scout initiation, at 7 years old. My mother was the Brownie Scout Leader and she led us in a familiar recital around a mirror placed on the stage floor with plastic leaves wrapped around it. We were told to imagine the mirror as a pond in a forest.

Each of us had a turn to step forward. My mom turned us around saying,

"Twist me and turn me and show me an elf

I looked in the water and saw..."

Then, it was our big moment. One by one we would straighten up, look into the "water" and say we saw,

"Myself!"

Amid a lot of cheering, we would have our pin put on upside down on our vest. Once we did three good turns, our family would get to turn the pin right side up.

Such a simple ceremony that it is surprising it came floating up to the surface of my mind for this introduction. And, yet, it seems an apt metaphor for our lives. It was my mother, the most familiar person, who initiated me. Suspension of belief into a consensus consciousness that we were not really on a stage, after hours, in our auditorium but in the woods, looking into a pond. For a young child, this was magic. But, it did feel real. The twisting and turning, all the while reciting a poem we practiced many times. But, this time we were opening a portal. Because, how many times in our young lives had we looked into a mirror. And, we all know a mirror shows us ourselves. What was the mystery and magic behind this looking? Why were we surprised to see ourselves? An elf?

So many mysteries to enjoy and participate in! Finally, the cheering and the pin turned backward – by an adult! And, we had quests to achieve so that our public display of membership would announce we performed three good deeds in a week. Very elemental, and almost leprechaun-ish. And brownies, are another name for woodland and house sprites. It all tied into a magic ceremony surrounding a central theme – who are we really?

A second image which came to my mind after writing the title of this chapter happened very recently to me. I was on the Reiki table with a number of practitioners giving me a few minutes of hands-on work during a Reiki Circle. I felt myself go into a very deep state.

In my mind's eye I saw a long rectangular shape, as a flower pod with a seam down the middle, floating right above my body. The top of the flower pod began peeling back. I watched, fascinated, as the unpeeling continued until about 1/3 down my body. The most beautiful light started emerging from the opening. It floated up a little and had the outline and indication of a humanoid with a round circle shape for a head and the silhouette of an upper body. The entire shape was luminous and shimmering.

I remember thinking, "Let me try to pull off the remainder of the covering so I can see the whole form."

'Hearing' inner laughter I got the impression or message that if I did that I would step out completely and this was not the time!

"Wait a minute! Is this me? Is this what I look like? Is this me in energy form?" Silence.

It was quite a vision and one that is still with me. Who are we really?

# Chapter 8 Overview

Below you will find 33 impressions for you to reflect upon and call upon when needed for encouragement and support. They are presented alphabetically for ease of finding, but, I recommend you read over the list and pick one or two to work on at a time. EnJoy browsing!

# Section 26

## Guideposts

The next few pages serve as guideposts on our journey.

To stay with our Light, our wisdom, and our deep longing to serve as Lightworkers, we read the signposts left to us by others. These others are the luminaries in the field. Perhaps, in past lives, we are serving as our own ancestors, reaching across time and space to remind ourselves of the Truth and offer helping hands when the journey is rough and the night is stormy.

## 33 Guideposts

1. Ability and Responsibility
2. All is Well
3. Appropriate Boundaries
4. Ascension Symptoms
5. Broadcast, Reception, Frequency
6. Clarity, Precision, Discernment
7. Connect with Apprentice Lightwork Community
8. Connect with Global Lightworkers
9. Connect with Light Grid
10. Cubbyhole Retreat
11. Daily Incarnation and
12. Dedication and Service
13. Drama Free: Minimize and Distract
14. The Game, part 1: Find the Gift
15. The Game, part 2: Razor's Edge Path
16. The Game, part 3: Don't Take It Personally
17. Go Higher to a Soul Perspective
18. Hero's Journey Part 1: Trapped Under the Story
19. Hero's Journey Part 2: Living at the Story Line Level
20. Hero's Journey Part 3: Arising Above the Story
21. Highest and Greatest Good for All

22. Inner Compass, Spiritual Will
23. Intent
24. Keep Focusing
25. Kindness, Compassion, Forgiveness for Oneself
26. Meditation and Mindfulness
27. Perfectly Imperfect
28. Read the Signs, Impeccably
29. Sacred Heart, Sacred Mind
30. Shift Happens
31. Stringing Pearls
32. Take Good Care of Yourself
33. Take Yourself Lightly

Take time to reflect on each of these areas. EnJoy the process, the journey and the destination of living in joy and shining our light!

## Ability and Responsibility

We have the ability to do this work. We have the ability to walk through multidimensional portals and create healing spaces for ourselves and others. We have the ability to connect through time and space and to interpret intuitive communications.

We also have the responsibility to be pristine in our work. We have the responsibility to have ethical and moral boundaries in place, to safeguard our client's privacy, and to walk humbly and confidently, both, on this path.

1. How do you show your ability and your responsibility?

_____

_____

_____

_____

_____

_____

_____

_____

_____

_____

_____

_____

_____

## All is Well

"All is well" is a common mantra, often sung, to remind us of this truth. If truly "all is well", then how is it we experience dis-ease, despair, depression, dissolution?

Vibrating the energy behind "all is well" is the key to understanding this life.

2. Do you notice a difference when you sing, chant, or say as a mantra, "all is well"? Do you believe all is well?

_____

_____

_____

_____

_____

_____

_____

_____

_____

_____

_____

_____

_____

_____

_____

## Appropriate Boundaries

As we grow and develop, our ability to boundary ourselves in our cocoon of light shifts and changes all the time. Appropriate boundaried envelopes, permeable to All There Is, joyously interpreting and broadcasting messages and connections, are protective when need be. Scan your energy field or aura. The majority of Lightworkers have 'shredded boundaries' which have been affected by trauma. I envision this as delicate cat claws shredding a sheer curtain. With shredded boundaries you are at the mercy of your surroundings, feeling too much, sinking in others' gravity wells.

A smaller percentage of Lightworkers have armored boundaries, hardened calluses, again from facing onslaughts of attacks. Instead of becoming shredded, our envelopes harden in places. It's fatiguing to be armored, and it's hard to take the armor off! Appropriate boundaries are light. They are protective but they also are permeable allowing us to be soft when appropriate and embracing of ourselves when appropriate.

3.  Scan your boundaries. Need any polishing?

_____

_____

_____

_____

_____

_____

_____

_____

_____

_____

_____

## Ascension Symptoms

If you take as a working model that 2012 is the midpoint of the precession of the equinoxes, a 26,000 year cycle, then we are in shift energies. We are ascending out of 3D, past 4D which is also known as an astral realm, and into 5D or multidimensional consciousness.

The Earth is vibrating faster, there are cycles of strong solar wind activities, and we are traveling in a part of space that we haven't passed through before while humans were on planet. It takes about 250 million years for our solar system to have one full revolution around the galactic center. Astrophysicists state that we do not travel in a circle, but weave up and down the galactic plane, bobbing about 250 light years above and below the galactic plane. We are also beginning to leave behind a field of thick galactic dust.

Vibrationally, things are quickening. And, our bodies need time to adjust to these fluctuating environmental/celestial changes. You might feel tired, dizzy, spaced out, have mood swings, altered sleep patterns, changes in jobs and relationships, and feelings of loneliness. I have had dizziness, blurred vision, ringing in my ears, heart palpitations off and on for a few years. Doctors have not been able to find anything wrong. Once I realized that it was probably ascension symptoms, they began to abate and then disappear. Rest, take yourself and the symptoms lightly – but check in with a doctor to be sure.

As you settle into a higher vibratory rate, you will begin to feel at peace, joyful, accepting. You will have more ease of manifesting, engaging relationships, evolving out of drama and lack, and release of old blocks. You might feel that you are living a new life, with heightened intuition and profound gratitude for this life adventure. Be ready and aware of these and don't wonder what happened – You happened!

4. Are you experiencing ascension symptoms? How are you handling them?

_____

_____

_____

_____

_____

_____

_____

_____

## Broadcast, Reception, Frequency

We know, from our quantum physicists, that we are energy beings, with possible 'super strings' vibrating at a sub-atomic level informing everything we see in the observable universe. Fun!

So, we are vibrating at our own unique frequency. According to Abraham-Hicks we are 'vibrational interpreters in a vibrational universe'. What are you broadcasting? What are you receiving?

5.  Do you know what you are broadcasting? What frequency ranges are you receiving? Do you believe this is possible to consciously tune in and tune out?

_____

_____

_____

_____

_____

_____

_____

_____

_____

_____

_____

_____

_____

_____

## Clarity, Precision, Discernment

It is important in our work to have clarity about what we are doing. Be precise and compassionate in sharing information with a client. Go to a higher level to get clarity of information for yourself and others. Rely on your inner wisdom and understandings, Old Soul, and use discernment before adding tools or methods, thinking these will finally allow you to step forward as a healer or Lightworker. Use discernment before giving your power away in readings. Learn to read for yourself and ask for guidance for your highest destiny path.

6.  How do clarity, precision, and discernment work in your life?

_____

_____

_____

_____

_____

_____

_____

_____

_____

_____

_____

_____

_____

_____

_____

## Connect with Apprentice Lightworker Community

There are levels of connecting with a Lightworker Community. This is the first level – connecting with Apprentices, giving and getting feedback from them on Reiki and intuitive skills. We are all together on this voyage and it is meant for each of us to be here, sharing our unique voices, perspectives, and gifts with each other. Build and expand your personal Lightworker community!

7.  What are you doing to connect with this Lightworker Community? Who are you aligning with the most? What gift is each person offering you?

_____

_____

_____

_____

_____

_____

_____

_____

_____

_____

_____

_____

_____

_____

_____

_____

## Connect with Global Lightworker Community

The second level of connecting with a community is with the Global Lightworkers. There are millions of people around the world who are sharing in this vision of bringing peace and harmony to earth. There are millions of people who have Reiki and want to send healing energies to global situations. Kryon has said that it only takes 1/2 of 1% to affect change. For a population of 7 billion people, that is 35 million people to bring wonderful, tolerant, equitable, loving, compassionate changes to our beloved jewel of a planet. And, with the both of us in place, that is only 34, 999, 998 people to go!

8. Make it a practice to call upon the Global Lightworker Community. Send to global situations. Identify as a Global Lightworker! What areas, people, animals, or situations call to you?

_____

_____

_____

_____

_____

_____

_____

_____

_____

_____

_____

_____

_____

## Connect with Light Grid

This third level of connecting is with Beings on the Light Grid. This is a system of lights surrounding our beautiful Earth. Each light is a Luminary Being, showering grace and unconditional love onto us all.

Vision this grid and take your rightful place on the gridwork, showering down your understandings, your unconditional love onto the planet. Know that you are seen, acknowledged, welcomed, and honored for your work on the Light Grid!

9.  Connect with this high vibratory Light Grid. Here you will find Archangels Michael, Raphael, Gabriel, Uriel, Metatron, and others. You will find high octaves of Jesus, Mary, the Magdala, Buddha, Quan Yin, Avolokitshevara, St. Germaine, Hilarion, Perfect Masters through the ages and countless others. Work side by side with these Luminous Beings – everyone is needed!

_____

_____

_____

_____

_____

_____

_____

_____

_____

_____

_____

_____

## Cubbyhole Retreat

We all have our secret spaces that we retreat to when things are hard, boring, upsetting, or drama filled. Some of our cubbyholes might be innocuous and safe zones for us. Others are more danger filled. Cubbyholes can be viewed positively as survival skills, and we can even be grateful for them. Some of mine are phone games, reading mysteries, watching TV and running stories. Increasing our 'muscles' to hold conscious intent longer, and to maintain a stronger Lightworker identity is important as we manifest more of who we are without sacrificing our breathing spaces.

10. Are you aware of your 'cubbyholes'? Are they helping you to balance or taking time and energy from what you love?

_____

_____

_____

_____

_____

_____

_____

_____

_____

_____

_____

_____

_____

_____

## Daily Incarnation & Nightly Ensoulment

As spirit- made- flesh, there is often benefit from having a transition time as you wake and start your day and as you prepare to fall asleep. As young children we hustle in the mornings to get ready for school, dressing, eating, and getting into the car or bus; and this lasts for years. Same goes for work schedules, and this lasts for decades. We are buffered from a conscious transition to our daily incarnations. The same is true with night routines, and, perhaps, bouts of insomnia clouding our nightly journeying and deep rejuvenation.

Sacralizing our daily incarnation and nightly ensouling helps us maintain a rhythm and wave.

11. Do you have a daily routine or celebration for day and night rhythms? If not, what one thing can you add right now?

_____

_____

_____

_____

_____

_____

_____

_____

_____

_____

_____

_____

_____

## Dedication and Service

As Lightworkers, everything we face in our lives can be part of a larger pattern, fractal, and measure of the human experience. We are living at a time when service surrounds us, even if only on the energy sending level. Waiting in line at a store driving you antsy? Time to send energy of gratitude for the availability of stores, and to those who live in 'food deserts' in America, where they get 'food' from gas stations and convenience stores. Exhausted from working, dinner, dishes, and dragging to get up tomorrow to do the same thing? Time to send energy to those who have it harder than we do – single parents with more children than we have, working longer hours with less pay. Or send to those who can't find a job and wander aimlessly and anxiously through their days.

12. Are you finding it easier to see your particular life circumstances from a larger perspective? Are you sending energy to expansive patterns?

_____

_____

_____

_____

_____

_____

_____

_____

_____

_____

_____

_____

_____

## Drama Free: Minimize and Distract

We live in a drama filled world. Life is challenging on many levels. As Lightworkers, we are very sensitive to harsh environments, people, and energies. To remove ourselves more and more from constant dread and drama, work with your thoughts to minimize the issue. Not everything is life and death. And even life and death is not really what we think it is.

Minimize is different than denial. We are not denying an occurrence, we are minimizing its effects on us and on our lives. Distract yourself from constantly ruminating over it. Practice holding the reins of your wild horses (thoughts) and every time your thought goes 'there', distract. Practice until you know the subtle differences between distract and deny. Free of the clutches of drama, hyperbole, and exaggerated offense, we can move forward, shining our Light.

13. What drama have you minimized and distracted yourself from today? How is it going?

_____

_____

_____

_____

_____

_____

_____

_____

_____

_____

_____

_____

_____

## The Game, part 1: Find the Gift

However challenging the circumstance – there is a gift hidden within. It reminds me of a geode, which is a stony, rough stone. Slice it open and there is a spectacular crystalline art form within. You can never tell the beauty hiding inside an ugly container. So, too, our lives, sometimes. Find the gift.

14. Can you remember a time or two when something happened and you were able to find a gift inside?

_____

_____

_____

_____

_____

_____

_____

_____

_____

_____

_____

_____

_____

_____

_____

## The Game, Part 2: Razor's Edge Path

Making our way through circumstances calls for the trapeze artist within. We walk a fine line between intent, purpose, and our desired outcome, and acceptance, surrender, and relief. Consider it to be as easy and effortless as an in-breath and out-breath. Breathing in we set our intent, breathing out we surrender and release.

15. Choose a life event you are experiencing right now. Walk the high wire or razor's edge path of intent and surrender. How does it feel?

_____

_____

_____

_____

_____

_____

_____

_____

_____

_____

_____

_____

_____

_____

## The Game, Part 3: Don't Take It Personally

A final part of this triad of The Game (of Life) is to consider that your experience is a collective human experience. Don't take it personally, or make it your personal cross, or badge. It is part of the whole, and we all experience the full banquet of experiences, especially Old Souls (you!).

16. Can you consider something you have experienced that can easily be expanded to a collective one?

_____

_____

_____

_____

_____

_____

_____

_____

_____

_____

_____

_____

_____

_____

## Go Higher to a Soul Perspective

Things look messy on the ground level. Think of a blight of a neighborhood, or a clear-cut forest, or scenes from a wreck, natural or man- made. Sometimes messes in our lives look pretty bad. Go up higher into a helicopter to survey the damage. Still looks bad, but you are slightly removed from the wreckage. Go higher onto an airplane, flying at 35,000 feet high. Earth looks pretty wonderful from that height. Still not convinced? Go higher still onto a space shuttle and view the wonder and majesty. Go higher!

17. Can you see a personal challenge from a higher perspective?

_____

_____

_____

_____

_____

_____

_____

_____

_____

_____

_____

_____

_____

_____

## Hero's Journey Part 1: Trapped Under the Story

As part of our unique Hero's Journey, we live the stories of our lives. Sometimes, we get so caught up in the story, we forget that we are also the writer, director, producer, cast, crew, audience, and reviewer. When we are 'under the story' we forget who we truly are and believe we are a victim, or a villain, or a vamp.

Yes, our stories are magnificent, even though we only see such a small part of them here in 3D. And, a lot of our stories don't seem to make sense to us. But, they are the stories of our life and we are method actors, deep in our roles. And, in this first take, we are suffering in the midst of a horror, thriller, suspense, or too-much-action movie.

18. What story lines are you enmeshed in and suffering through at this time?

_____

_____

_____

_____

_____

_____

_____

_____

_____

_____

_____

_____

_____

## Hero's Journey Part 2: Living at Story Line Level

A continuation of our life story, level 2 brings us to the level of the story as a vehicle for expression. We are still immersed in the story, but we can take breaks, go home, relax a little, before we have to get up at 3 or 4 am and get back to the set, putting on our make-up and costumes, and diving into our roles again.

Here, we are still embedded in the story, but we recognize it is a story and that it could be changed. Why, oh why, are we in a horror movie? We hate horror movies. Or, we hate that we are in a lost-love movie, or a tale of brokenness and redemption. Just as the movies we pay to see, there are basic universal themes that go around and around.

We know there is a story being played, and we sometimes step off the set. We are at the level of the story line.

19. What parts of your unique Hero's Journey life story are you aware that you are playing a role? How long can you stay out of the story? What triggers you back in?

_____

_____

_____

_____

_____

_____

_____

_____

_____

_____

_____

_____

# Hero's Journey Part 3: Arising Above the Story

The trinity completion for our story metaphor, here we are watching and acting in our story, but we are aware that we are also the director, and the writer, the producer. We can change the script at any time. We are also the audience and critic, so we sit back and enjoy the tale. And, give ourselves great reviews!

We are above the story. We are enjoying the experience. We slip in and out of our true identities easily and effortlessly, enjoying all of it.

20. Are you arising above your story?

_____

_____

_____

_____

_____

_____

_____

_____

_____

_____

_____

_____

_____

_____

## Highest and Greatest Good for All

This is a stronger perspective on 'All is Well'. Not only is all well, but we are consciously intending that we intend the Highest and Greatest Good for All. When something happens that is not what we hoped for, if it is Highest and Greatest Good that we set a prayer and intent, and vibrated towards, without resistance, then what occurs is Highest and Greatest Good. Next step might be to open to see the gift, to see how that is greatest good.

And, if it is Highest and Greatest Good for All, then it cannot be good for one person and bad for another. It's for all. Again, you may have to work yourself upwards towards an understanding of how that could be, given your perspective.

There is peace and acceptance in this energy, as well as conscious intent and purity of agenda. Yes, we might want a particular outcome, but we are also open to an even better one, or, to understanding and trusting that this outcome, unexpected as it may be, is the highest and greatest good for all.

21. Intend Highest and Greatest Good for All when you are facing an upcoming decision or challenge. Then monitor how the situation unfolded. If not to your expectations, how can you go higher to see the larger perspective?

_____

_____

_____

_____

_____

_____

_____

_____

_____

_____

_____

## Inner Compass, Spiritual Will

Visualize, and then feel, an inner compass within you. It is built in and works all the time. This compass always lets us know what direction points home. There is a sense of relief, acceptance, joy, grace, and unconditional love. There is a strength within us, a spiritual willpower that has brought us this far. Trust in your inner compass, trust in your spiritual willpower.

22. Can you remember when you felt lost, alone, frightened? How did you find your way home?

_____

_____

_____

_____

_____

_____

_____

_____

_____

_____

_____

_____

_____

_____

_____

_____

## Intent

Holding a strong intent is vital for Lightworkers, even if the intent is to shine light and love on yourself, your life, and others. Abraham Hicks gives many examples of having intent - my favorite is visualizing wanting to drive from Portland to Seattle. You are driving north, then get off at an exit, get turned around, and go back on the parkway in the wrong direction. Still want to go to Seattle? Then you need to turn around, get onto the right lane in the right direction, and you will eventually get there.

Not sure where you're going? Hard to get there! Perhaps start with asking for help, asking for what you need to know today. And, pray, highest and greatest good for all!

23. Where do you want to go?

_____

_____

_____

_____

_____

_____

_____

_____

_____

_____

_____

_____

_____

## Keep Focusing

Although this seems commonsense, it is often hard to keep your focus on shining your light. Mad at someone? Feel betrayed? Lonely? Want a relationship or more abundance in your life? Keep focusing. Lost your way, got sidetracked? Haven't practiced any energy tools or techniques for a while? So what? Focus again with no judgment, only compassion and unconditional love for yourself. Jump on board and focus!

24. How do you remind yourself to focus?

_____

_____

_____

_____

_____

_____

_____

_____

_____

_____

_____

_____

_____

_____

## Kindness, Compassion, Forgiveness for Oneself

We are much kinder to others than we are to ourselves. We forgive others more easily than we forgive ourselves. We are able to show other mercy and compassion much more than we do ourselves. Lightworker, shine love, gentleness, kindness, respect and honor on yourself!

25. How often do you show kindness, compassion and forgiveness to yourself? Is there a certain area, or situation that consistently calls for you to heal?

_____

_____

_____

_____

_____

_____

_____

_____

_____

_____

_____

_____

_____

_____

## Meditation & Mindfulness

Meditation is the act of going within. It is challenging to sit with the contents of one's mind and to be constantly reminded in the space of a few minutes that we have very little control over what we are thinking. Our mind follows highways and byways of its own connections and many times we are hurled along for the ride. Nowhere is this more evident than when we make efforts to go within ourselves. We push past boundaries of mind, and of boredom, itchiness, forgotten things that must be done Now! It is worth it. We begin to slow down and enter a numinous, expansive and connected state of consciousness. We can sit in meditation, walk in meditation, repeat phrases or mantras, there are so many ways to stop the mind and enter the portal within.

Mindfulness has roots in meditation, but is more of a western adaptation, currently very popular in physical and mental health spheres. In mindfulness, one does not attempt to go beyond mind but to accept mind, sensations, thoughts, and feelings without judgment. The attempt is to be present in the moment and be accepting.

26. Do you have a daily practice of meditation or mindfulness? A daily practice does not need to be long or complex. Connecting within and being present in the moment are two very powerful inner tools! What can you introduce into your daily life right now?

_____

_____

_____

_____

_____

_____

_____

_____

_____

_____

_____

## Perfectly Imperfect

We are imperfect, we know this very well. And, yet, we all strive to be perfect and not make any mistakes. No one likes to make mistakes, but, in striving for perfection, something we cannot reach, we miss the gift that we are actually perfect in our imperfections. On the opposite spectrum is the throw-away that "oh well, that's just the way I am. I'm not going to change." Really? Why? We change all the time, even down to our cells and organs. We can and do change our minds and feelings. Ever feel shock you felt undying love for someone you can't bear to ever look at again?

Why not change our perfect imperfections, balancing them out, smoothing out the roughnesses, and then allowing another perfection- in- imperfection to manifest?

27. How do you know you are perfectly imperfect? How can you rejoice in your humanity as spirit made flesh?

_____

_____

_____

_____

_____

_____

_____

_____

_____

_____

_____

_____

## Read the Signs, Impeccably

We work with an intelligently guided universe and swim in waters filled with life in all dimensions. When we are in a vulnerable state, perhaps we look for signs? Sometimes they are so visible, literally at our feet (penny, feather). Other times we open and ask for information (oracle cards, prayers). And, then there are times that we desperately grab at straws to find or fashion a sign when we are in a wait-and-see space (he loves me, he loves me not, choosing card after card till you get one you like, psychic readings).

Reading signs is a wonderful, intuitive activity. It heightens and enlightens us. Another spectrum to this is losing our sense of free agency as we become superstitiously shackled by outside forces, demanding the 'right' answer. There is a sweet spot between standing in your empowerment, asking, and reading signs and desperately gyrating to come up with answers we want. It's called being impeccable. And that's a gift of ours, Lightworker.

28. Do you have instances when you correctly obtained guided information? Do you have instances when you desperately forced 'information' which disempowered you?

_____

_____

_____

_____

_____

_____

_____

_____

_____

_____

_____

_____

## Sacred Heart, Sacred Mind

There is a sweet synergy between heart and mind, between the higher octaves of our heart song and the creative sparks of our boundless mind. It is a dance between the two and it helps us find our way, and it helps us light up so that others may find their way as well. Uncovering a deep devotional love with the Beloved is a gift and a joy, and you can dance for infinity with this ecstatic marriage.

29. What does sacred heart/sacred mind mean to you?

_____

_____

_____

_____

_____

_____

_____

_____

_____

_____

_____

_____

_____

_____

_____

## Shift Happens

A playful play on words, it is good to remember two things. The first is that we are in shift energies. Some describe it as moving past the 2012 midpoint of the precession of the equinoxes. Others say we are moving from the age of darkness to a golden age of peace, or that we are moving from the age of Pisces to the age of Aquarius. I've also heard it said we are moving from 3rd to 5th dimension, ascending, or moving from homo sapiens to homo luminens. Utilizing this particular model of reality (because, why not?), it is good to remember that this too, shall pass. And, it will change for the better. Trust in this!

Lightworker, look past the detritus, chaos and confusion of the dying age and shine light on the possibilities!

30. Considering this view of reality, consider how awe inspiring it is that we have chosen to incarnate at this particular time in this particular culture to do our Lightwork! We are worker bees!  What visions do you hold of this shift time?

_____

_____

_____

_____

_____

_____

_____

_____

_____

_____

_____

_____

_____

_____

## Stringing Pearls

As Lightworkers, we shoulder and heal burdens in our lives, we encounter and heal challenging issues and relationships, and we experience joy and gratitude for heartfelt occurrences. And, all this is a life's blessing.

But, why stop there? Elevate those experiences and set your markers for healing, completion, joy, gratitude and blessings in the grid of time and space for others to see and grab in times of peril, darkness, hopelessness, and fullness. I call this 'stringing pearls' as it appears as a string of lights (pearls) and also adds to the web of all life experiences (Indra's net).

As you consciously walk your path, fulfilling your chosen activities and destinies, string pearls for others to light their way. And, dance!

31. Consciously send one of your present challenges or joy upward and outwards to the web of life, stringing pearls. What are you stringing? How does it feel?

_____

_____

_____

_____

_____

_____

_____

_____

_____

_____

_____

_____

## Take Good Care of Yourself

As discussed under Ascension Symptoms, and as we know from life on earth with physical, mental, emotional, and existential challenges, as well adding on a good dose of pervasive toxicity of food, water, air, soil, chronic and acute stress, and 7 billion people writhing through global birthing pangs – we need to remember our self-care! Have a well formed self-care tool kit of 20, 30 or more ways to care for yourself physically, mentally, emotionally, socially, creatively, energetically, and spiritually.

32. How does your self-care tool kit look? Anything you would like to add to it?

_____

_____

_____

_____

_____

_____

_____

_____

_____

_____

_____

_____

_____

_____

_____

## Take Yourself Lightly

In 7th grade I had to make a speech on an author and I chose, randomly, G.K. Chesterton. I had never read anything of his, but a library book caught my imagination. "On laying in bed", "Homesick at home", "What I found in my pocket" ... who knew English literature authors could be so whimsical? Imagine my surprise when I googled who wrote the quote to this ending of our conscious identification?

"Angels fly because they take themselves lightly."  G.K. Chesteron

Let us take ourselves and each other lightly, and, let us fly!

33. Have you had dreams of flying? Do you want to fly? How do you Lighten up?

_____

_____

_____

_____

_____

_____

_____

_____

_____

_____

_____

_____

_____

_____

# Summary of Chapter 8

What areas are easy for you? What areas are you finding challenging right now?

_____

_____

_____

_____

_____

_____

_____

_____

_____

_____

_____

_____

_____

_____

_____

*The present of the Presence is the presence of the
Present!*

# Chapter 9

# Quantum

# Quirks

# Stepping into the Quantum World

The chapter is a light reflection on deep dimensions. More of this discussion is in Book 9 of the Tools for Lightworkers Series, *Arise: A Soul Based Perspective on Counseling and Healing.*

Quantum physics has been with us for almost 120 years – and it is just within the last decade that it has begun to make its way into our understanding of reality. Mathematicians and theoretical physicists have been playing in the quantum for over a century, trying to wrap their minds around it. But, that is the problem. Everyday mental structures cannot wrap around quantum. We need to expand our mental/energetic 'quantum perceptors' to play in the quantum.

Every time there is a major shift in our worldview, there is much jockeying for power, ownership, and professional discourtesies. Every field has gone through this sorry state of miserly adding to our knowledge base, because 'experts' believe they own the one and only current viewpoint in their field. Therefore, this hoarding of information by keeping quantum solely with the physics and mathematical realms, is not new.

In 1900 Lord Kelvin, a renowned physicist, said 'we now know everything there is to know in physics. All that remains is to measure things.' And, he said it just before general relativity and quantum mechanic revolutions hit the field, changing it forever. More recently, in 1998, physicists again thought they had the universe pretty well understood, until 'dark matter' (27%) and 'dark energy' (68%) was confirmed by two teams of astrophysicists. 'Dark' meaning unknown, everything observable in the universe clocks in at a mere 5%! Everything observable! We are living in a Renaissance of science and consciousness and can't see within our own bubble.

# Chapter 9 Overview

We will discuss many of these topics and there are wonderful reference materials available for you to read while you swing in hammocks, allowing your constructs of reality to be transformed and freed from older shackles. We then travel through this realm to play with quantum inner dynamics and healing techniques. EnJoy the unknowing uncertainty, possible probables and mystic magic of working and living in the Quantum!

Section 27 gives a short overview of quantum quirks. We start with the quick question, "What is reality?" and move on gathering perspectives.

There are volumes of books to read and hundreds of videos to watch about the sub-atomic world and the unique configuration of the quantum. There are also wonderful esoteric understandings of working in the quantum by many pioneering authors and, yes, even scientists. Lee Carroll is an excellent esoteric guide through the quantum. When we work with quantum principles and theories, we more clearly grasp, albeit intuitively, the engine driving healing and energy work!

Section 28, Quantum Consciousness, allows us to wander through the quantum, visiting friend and foe alike, in the Archetypal Forest. There is also an excerpted, haunting, poem by Rumi included.

In Section 29 we visit Angelic and Soul Ray names which have been given for past Apprentices. These lineage lines open new avenues within us for expansion and glimpsing more of who we truly are. There is space to add our community of Lightworkers to the list.

Finally, in Section 30, there is a guided visualization and meditation for expanded chakras and a beautiful illustration of the Conscious Human Tree, expanded between heaven and earth.

EnJoy the quirky, mind-bending reality of quantum travels!

# Section 27

## Quantum Fun and Models of Reality

What is reality?

How do you know what is real? Worldviews on the basis of reality have changed tremendously over the millennia. People believed in gods and goddesses, witches and demons, harmonic spheres circling around a central Earth, and, even currently for a few people, flat earths.

Fairly recently, people thought the Milky Way was the entirety of the universe. Our sense of what is real and what is not is constantly shifting and changing.

Here are some of the fascinating quantum quirks:

1.  What we see is what we get.

    We cannot examine anything in the quantum without changing it, just by our observation. Waves become particles through observation, or consciousness. With no observation or consciousness present, particles present as waves. Seeing something changes that potential or wave into a particle or substance. This is the engine behind the idea that we create our own reality. What you focus on, appears in your field (Law of Attraction)

2.  Solid matter is mostly empty space.

    If you collapse the Empire State Building into actual matter, you would end up with a grain of rice – an extremely heavy grain. All the rest of the Empire State Building is empty space! We are mostly empty space. Or, seemingly empty space. There is no mass involved but there are energy fields holding the template.

    Turns out that ancient Hindu texts and mystics across the ages have been right. Everything is 'maya' or illusion. It all appears real, sense oriented, tested, and verifiable. And, yet, everything is huge expanses of empty space! If an atom were the size of a football field, the nucleus, containing the mass of the atom would be the size of a flea in the middle of the field! The world looks solid, but it is waves of energy, with us, as consummate perceptors and interpreters, making a world out of 'thin air'.

3.  Science is on the verge of proving everything is connected.

    There are fields around everything from sub-atomic level to galaxies. There is also a universal field, known to physicists as 'non-locality' and 'entangled fields'. Until the waves of energy solidify into a particle, an electron is everywhere at once, according to quantum mechanics. With this idea of non-locality and entangled fields,, everything is connected. A paired particle, separated across the universe, will instantaneously change when it's paired partner changes.

    We are all connected regardless of time, space, or distance. Putting this universal field, with consciousness behind, within, and in front of all manifestations sounds a lot like 'universal life force energy' or the Rei of Reiki.

4.  We create our own reality.

    Opposed to a finite, determined, sole truth, quantum allows for subjective, personal truths, with overlapping realities. The universe is filled with possibilities and probabilities. Recently, a physicist, d'Espagnat, has declared that consciousness itself creates our physical world. 'Superposition' means that anything is possible! An electron is in all positions. We create, from our subconscious mind, our thoughts and feelings, our own individual world.

    Similarly, time and space are not what we perceive them to be. Therefore, we can create within our own reality and also go back and forth in time or space or dimension to set energies in place. It is done with intent, focus, practice, strong motivation, grace – but it is absolutely possible. Medical science has documented spontaneous healings of every kind of dis-ease imaginable and placebos are one of the most powerful medical healings, accounting for 50, 60, even in some research 75% of remission.

    And, in the quantum, things don't happen in steps. They happen immediately.

5.  We are stardust – literally.

    The elements that go into making our bodies (and everything we see) come from exploding stars. We are also frozen light – literally, according to quantum physicist, David Bohm. As Lightworkers, we intuitively know that we are light. Our scientists also 'know' this as well.

6. Quantum physics defines WHY energy healing works!

There are infinite levels of probabilities. Schrodinger's cat is both alive and dead. Even with past events, we are able, through energy healing techniques, to move between quantum possibility doorways.

Conventional medicine believes in 'scientific materialism' and the medical field is based still in Newtonian worldviews. But there are a few in the medical field who are working with the newer quantum paradigm.

Rupert Sheldrake, an eminent British biologist, and originator of the concept of 'morphic resonance' or fields, has been called a 'scientific heretic' and 'renegade biologist'. His recent book *The Science Delusion/Science Set Free* is a fascinating read for anyone interested in the trajectory of science and medicine.

Other medical 'renegades' include Bruce Lipton, a developmental biologist who posits that genes and DNA can be influenced by thoughts and emotions. Candace Pert, a neuroscientist and pharmacologist who discovered opiate receptors and neuropeptides wrote on integrating science with holistic energy medicine.

We are on the cresting wave!

## Quantum Healing

In 1687 Isaac Newton wrote *Principia Mathematica* and detailed 3 laws of motion. He demonstrated that the world (our reality) is logical, predictable, based upon observation and common sense. This has come to be known as determinism, materialism, and the scientific method. The universe, according to Newton, works as a giant machine, ticking along its determined path. Anything outside this view is seen as superstition or illusion. There is a single truth of reality, and scientists discover this reality by being neutral observers.

This worldview – determined, mechanistic – reached its highpoint in the last century as psychology (ironically, from Greek, psychology means the study of the soul) transduced human beingness to behaviors solely, with disdain and complete professional scorn for the actual study of the soul. All of that is changing with the quantum worldview seeping out of the fingers of physicists and mathematicians and into the social scientists, philosophers (the ancient forerunners of all sciences), and, happily enough, energy healers.

Quantum quirks give energy healers the trappings of the engine which drives energy healing. We work within the quantum possibilities, working with waves of potential, in the interconnected field, as we work with clients to set energetic healing structures for themselves. And, this can be done instantaneously, even chronic conditions and situations, as we move between time, space and dimension.

Physicists have unwittingly become the metaphysicians of our time! Not that they are taking this crowning lightly. In actuality, they are holding fast to the strands of their realities and are aghast at those of us in the energy field who are grasping the true nature of reality behind their experiments. Which is ironic, as probably many energy healers work with intuition and guidance, not with mathematical engines driving the way forward.

There are 7 quantum healing techniques detailed below:

1. Archetypes and Collective Unconscious
2. Hero's Journey
3. Inner Child
4. Wise Sage/ Angelic Self
5. Inner Landscapes
6. Divine Feminine /Divine Masculine
7. Shadow Self and Shadow Saboteur
8. Quantum Doorways

EnJoy the journeys!

# Section 28

## Quantum Travels

### Archetypes and Collective Unconscious

Archetypes were defined by both Carl Jung and Joseph Campbell. They are richly experienced inner patterns which we play with across all times and all cultures. They show up in religion, art, music, drama, and in our unconscious. These ancient and present themes are found in all our myths, stories, and lives.

Some examples of archetypes are the mother, lover, rebel, poet, saint, thief, hero, goddess, magician, healer, victim, villain, and redeemer. Carolyn Myss has written a book on archetypes called *Sacred Contracts* and also has published an Archetype card deck. In a fun exercise, Myss asks you to pair 12 of your major archetypes with an astrological house matrix. You choose 8 personal archetypes. According to Myss we all carry 4 communal ones: child, victim, saboteur, and prostitute. Interesting to consider.

1. Do you enjoy working with archetypes? What are some of your main archetypes?

_____

_____

_____

_____

_____

_____

_____

_____

_____

_____

_____

## Hero's Journey

There are a number of ways to consider the Hero's Journey and both Joseph Campbell and Carl Jung are two wonderful contributors to our knowledge of this dynamic construct. Drama, storytelling, myth, religion, psychological development, and spiritual journeying all merge in this perception of each of us being a Hero on a specific quest, adventure, journey.

One map of the Hero's Journey is 8 fold:

1. Birth
2. Growth
3. Withdrawal
4. Mentor, quest
5. Death
6. Underworld
7. Rebirth
8. Legacy

We travel through each of these areas developmentally, and also cyclically throughout our lives. It certainly helps in times of trial and crisis to reframe our perspective and understand that we truly are Hero's and that we truly are on a journey. This is the soul perspective.

As an archetype, the Hero is visioned by all cultures and myths. It is part of our own story and is part of what Jung has called the 'collective unconscious' or story for all the ages. Perhaps this could be known as the astral.

These 8 stages include some kind of unusual circumstances around birth (what were your birth circumstances?). The Hero grows and then an event causes some inward withdrawal or the hero copes with trauma. This leads to an adventure, a quest, and often finding a mentor. Sometimes the Hero has help, has supernatural qualities (so evident in comic heroes) and needs to prove themselves. There is usually 'death' or despair of some kind, and hard, inconsolable times of wandering, lost either externally or internally. Rebirth or resolution magically occurs and we see the lessons learned have rewards, for ourselves and others, in this life and 'happily ever after'.

2.  Where are you on the Hero's Journey? Do you see yourself as a Hero? Can you Not see yourself as a Hero? Write a summary of your life as a Hero!

_____

_____

_____

_____

_____

_____

_____

_____

_____

_____

_____

_____

_____

## Inner Child

Another wonderful archetype is Inner Child, our sweet, innocent young child from approximately 2 – 7 years old. Can you see yourself at that age?

The wonderful thing about working in the quantum is that time is not a factor so we can access the past as easily as the present. Your Inner Child lives with you now! How is s/he doing these days? Are you being a good parent to this precious child?

*Spectrum Energetics* works with our Inner Child. EnJoy the chance to protect, save, embrace, and unconditionally love and cherish this beautiful, innocent treasure.

3. For one or more of our personal sessions together, locate your Inner Child – what chakra are they living in? What messages do they have for you? What is it they need or want from you?

_____

_____

_____

_____

_____

_____

_____

_____

_____

_____

_____

_____

## Wise Sage/Angelic Self

As with Inner Child, there exists within our field the wise, connected, sacred part of ourselves, the Wise Sage or the Angel Guide. That Highest and Greatest part of who we truly are. The being we see in the True Mirror.

This archetype/quantum reality lives with us every moment. Are you listening?

4. What messages do your Wise Sage/ Angelic Self have for you today? What would you like to ask of the wise, all-knowing part of you?

_____

_____

_____

_____

_____

_____

_____

_____

_____

_____

_____

_____

_____

_____

_____

## Inner Landscapes

As real as our outer world, there exists inner landscapes within us. These are 'places' that reveal what we are going through and how they might look in a quantum terrain.

There are known places that many traverse – the lake of tears, the mountain of challenge, the void of how to get across the chasm; there are many!

In guided personal work, we access your immediate inner landscape and reveal an inner map for you to use as a tool to move forward in your life and your life's work. *Spectrum Energetics* also access this information for you.

5. For one or more of our personal sessions, focus on your immediate inner landscape and your quest. How do you like working in the quantum?

_____

_____

_____

_____

_____

_____

_____

_____

_____

_____

_____

_____

_____

_____

## Divine Feminine, Divine Masculine

Two more of our archetypes, the divine feminine and the divine masculine are wakening in our lifetimes. The Divine Feminine has been re-membered since the 1970's and 1980's with the work of so many wonderful researchers including *When God Was A Woman*, and *Ancient Mirrors of Womanhood*, by Merlin Stone, *The Languge of the Goddess* by Marija Gimbutas, and *The Spiral Dance* by Starhawk . Jean Shinoda Bolen, a Jungian therapist, has written 3 fun books including *Goddess in Everywoman, Gods in Everyman*, and **Goddesses in Older Women**. The *Woman's Wheel of Life* by Elilzabeth Davis and Carole Leonard is another wonderful reference book, bringing matriarch to the maiden, mother, crone mythos.

The Divine Masculine has yet to arise from the ashes of patriarchy, greed, corruption, power, and conquering mentality. The last few decades have seen many men, especially younger ones, work within the Divine Feminine arena and hold more gentle, communal, and relational energies. Yet, the Divine Masculine is preparing to rise. And, not a moment too soon!

The Divine Mother and the Divine Father are offshoots of this major archetype and, in the quantum, are wonderful to call upon for wisdom, strength, clarity and unconditional love.

The Goddess in particular has been invoked for a few decades. She is known throughout cultures and timespans and works with you on a full spectrum of issues. We are so blessed in Oregon to have as our state motto, "She flies with her own wings"!

6. Call upon these Divine Archetypes. What messages do they have for you?

_____

_____

_____

_____

_____

_____

_____

_____

_____

_____

## Shadow Self and the Shadow Saboteur

Bringing in the complementary shadow to our inner worlds is important in our world of polarity, good/bad, right/wrong, beauty/ugliness, and war/peace.

According to Carl Jung, the Shadow is an unconscious part of ourselves that the ego does not wish to be identified with. We isolate and try to keep our Shadow selves away from us, denying their power, resiliancy and juiciness to our wholeness. Apart from us, they may easily sabotage our movement forward. Embracing and loving the imperfect, and maybe the unlovable, parts of us is part of our journey.

Someone I know is a Gemini, known in astrological circles as the twins. He plays with his shadow by giving 'evil twin Sam' a different name than his own (John). When he does or says something to irritate others, he excuses himself by blaming the action on Sam. Funny, insightful, and somewhat self-accepting.

7. Consider shadow parts of yourself that you have split off from your main identity. Name them, call them in to visit. Can you embrace them?

_____

_____

_____

_____

_____

_____

_____

_____

_____

_____

_____

## The Guest House

*A joy, a depression, a meanness,*

*Welcome and entertain them all!*

*Even if they're a crowd of sorrows,*

*who violently sweep your house*

*still, treat each guest honorably.*

*The dark thought, the shame, the malice,*

*meet them at the door laughing,*

*and invite them in.*

*Be grateful for whoever comes,*

*because each has been sent as a guide from beyond.*

Excerpt from Rumi

(Translation by Coleman Barks)

## Quantum Doorways

A wonderful, subtle, yet powerful technique is to work within quantum doorways.

Working on the understanding of probabilities, possible realities, and the ability to go between time and space, you can set up a quantum doorway for any number of situations. To heal trauma in the past, to deal with remorse, grief, guilt, or other strong emotions about your past choices, put Cho Ku Rei on the ceilings (we are traveling between dimensions, buckle your 'seat belt' for protection).

Draw the Hon Sha Ze Sho Nen distant sending symbol and then vision a doorway, or two, or three. Use your intuitive senses. Say a Prayer of Intent. Then work within your guided visualization to see if you can open the door. Sometimes we are on the threshold, other times the door is present but locked. Most times the door swings open and we emerge ... into a parallel reality. Walk through and see what is different if you had made the opposite choice, or didn't experience the trauma that is still haunting you.

Feel the relief and lightness of this alternate reality. Intend to bring that wisdom and insight back with you into this 3D reality. You can come back and visit anytime. Or perhaps, you might merge both realities. You are the creator of your own experience.

Feel the healings which take place from living this alternate reality. For decision-making between 2 or more choices, open the 2 or 3 doors and see what each reality feels like. You will have a much better idea of the ramifications of your decision.

Finally, gift yourself some time to see the effects of this alternate reality and healing upon your life now. In my experience, it often brings relief, understanding of your (and others' choices), and compassion to yourself and all involved. It also can take a little time for the healing or resolution to 'bubble up' to your present life frame.

This method can also be considered for clients and is taught in all the advanced healing methods of the Lightworker Apprenticeship.

8.  Open a quantum doorway. What is your experience?

_____

_____

_____

_____

_____

_____

# Section 29

## SoulAnge Harmonics

An advanced energy healing technique uniquely designed and taught at Arise, SoulAnge Harmonics works with the Angelic or Soul Ray lineages for present and past Apprentices. Begun a few decades ago, I accessed my lineage, *Elorhaim Seraphim Magnificat*, and have worked with this gift, allowing it to enrich my practice and my life.

Below are some of the SoulAnge Harmonics given to Lightworkers and dearly cherished loves. After seeing a few that had the same 'surnames' I realized they are lineages from Source.

We also have DNA lineages from our family system, back through hundreds of thousands of years. National Geographic has a genomic project that can trace your ancient DNA routes out of Africa. Ancestry.com and other sites can trace the percentage of your ethnic heritages, which is a broad, not as deep lineage patterning.

A second type of lineage is soul based, where we can go through our Akash, or, trained in *Spectrum Energetics*, we can access past life information from the chakra system. This type of lineage is based upon soul incarnation.

SoulAnge is a third unique lineage line based upon your Soul Ray.

Below is a list of Arise Apprentices and their SoulAnge lineages.

*Can't wait to sing yours!*

# Apprentice SoulAnge Harmonic Lineage

| | |
|---|---|
| AoRhondular | Presence Within; Oceanic Presence (Tony) |
| Ariandelle | Elfin Meadow Song (Hillary) |
| Brala Mar | Beauty and Joy (Michelle) |
| Clara Sira Royale | Clear Sight (Norah) |
| Dri Lana Mar | Light drenched beauty (Amy) |
| Dulchinar Serene | Sweetness and serenity (Felicia) |
| Elorahim Seraphim Magnificat | The Song of Creation (Lorelynn) |
| Erandurille | Everlasting light, life, hope, strength (Diane) |
| Iromel Dinal | Straight from the heart, to the heart (Heidi) |
| Jai Ru Mala | Joyful bubbling laughter (Tyleena) |
| Kirianna Rhea Luna | Praise be; Light in the night (Beth) |
| Kore Ame | Deep Within; All resides, truth abides (Alex) |
| Morant'ha | Peace weaving, serpent wielding, scepter healing (Jeff) |
| Mubarek Erani | Inter-dimension traveler; Inner-d explorer (Merrill) |
| Reena Mareva | The (Beauty and) Wonder of it all! (Kristin) |
| Ruar Dinal | Roaring Sister, giving voice (Jodi) |
| Seremi Amor | Seremi Ador, Seremi Amor; Heart flame (Loraine) |

## Apprentice Soul Lineages:

# Section 30

This meditation came to me one night in 2016. I became conscious of a poem being recited to me and then moved into an expanded chakra meditation, where each chakra is linked galactically and cosmically.

I don't have much more information except to say that I feel very blessed to have gotten this 'transmission' and hope to get more. As I was writing this manual for you, months later, I once again dreamed part of the meditation with the addition that our sun was called Hapthor and the Milky Way was called Alcyzar. Have to love different and unique views of reality!

When you practice this expanded meditation, lie down and play some light music. Read through the progression first so you know the specific chakra which links to an expanded port. Begin and end with the poem/prayer.

EnJOY!

## Expanded Chakra Meditation

"Door Opening

Love emerging, life Beckoning

Miracles abounding, life is so astounding

Life Unending

On our knees bending"

Breath       Take 3 breaths, feeling the comfort and ease with breathing in just the right amount of air, without needing to force or pressure the breath. And feel the relief with breathing out just the right amount without forcing or pushing.

Ground       Now follow your breath down your body, down your legs and out the soles of your feet as if you have roots growing from you. They go down, down into the Earth, as far down as you feel comfortable. And anchor in there – feeling safe, secure, grounded, and protected.

1st       Focus upon your 1st chakra, the root chakra, which is located at the base of your torso. This chakra connects us to safety, security issues, to faith and trust in God and life, and to the lower half of our body. Now expand the connection from your 1st chakra into the core of the Earth, going into the heart of the crystal core center of the Earth, feeling Earth's pulse, her heartbeat, and the strength that comes from this elemental and telluric core. Breathe into this expanded 1st chakra.

2nd       Next we move up to your 2nd chakra, the relational chakra located just below the navel. The 2nd chakra connects us to our creativity, sexuality, relationships, love, unions and Inner Child. Feel this relational chakra expand to the envelope of skin that surrounds your body. Feel the embrace of the air against your envelope. Now breathe and expand further into your lightbody, visualizing your aura, mental, emotional, spiritual and energy fields expanding 3 to 6 to 12 feet outwards front and back, left and right, top and bottom. Here you are in your energy state. Breathe into this expanded 2nd chakra.

3rd        We move up to your 3rd chakra, located at your solar plexus. This chakra connects to the power and control in your life; this chakra is your identity center. Feel the connection with this chakra as we expand to the Gaia partnership, honoring the fullness of incarnating into physicality on Earth. Expand to encompass your home, your state, your country, your continent, and then the entire world. Expand further to the envelope of our atmosphere and a vision of our bejeweled planet spinning in the heavens. Breathe and expand again to include the Earth's magnetosphere, spiraling around our precious planet in protection and angel wings. Finally, connect your 3rd chakra to Earth's complete energy body and auric crown.

4th        We move up to our 4th chakra, our heart center. This chakra connects us to our heart and lungs, breathing life and love into everything we do. This chakra is also related to relationships and unions, to our deepest loves, and also to mercy, compassion, unconditional love and the Boddhisatva path. Breathe and expand a connection from your heart chakra to the heart of our Solar Angel, our Sun. Breathe in the warmth, light, and unconditional love from our Solar Angel. Expand further into the heliosphere of our Sun's solar wind and magnetic fields of information. Expand again as the solar influence continues past our planets, past the Kuiper belt, past the Oort cloud, the heliosheath and into the magnetic sheathing around our magnificent solar system as we spiral, embraced within the Orion Arm. Connect your heart center and 4th chakra to the magnificent solar landscape.

5th        Move up again to our 5th chakra, our throat center. The 5th chakra connects us to our communications, to speaking our truth and living our truth, living in pristine integrity. Breathe into this chakra and allow an expansive connection from our 5th chakra to the heart of the Mother, our Galactic Mother, the push/pull twin energies at the heart of our Milky Way Galaxy. Feel the connection we have to our Galactic Mother, the Sagittarius A star, and to all energies of hundreds of billions of stars within our magnificent spiraling galaxy as we breathe into our identity of galactic citizen.

6th        Moving up to our 6th chakra, our brow or 'third eye' chakra connects us to wisdom, knowledge, imagination, intuition and insight. Here we are connected to higher learning, the Hall of Records, higher perceptions and timeless wisdom. We breathe and expand the connection from our brow chakra moving beyond our galaxy and local stellar neighborhood and beyond the Laniakea Supercluster and directly into the heart of the Universe, the Father, the universal matrix grid, a billions of lightyears adventure. Here we connect to the heart of the cosmos and our cosmic conscious identity.

7th        "Door opening." (Use fingers to widen triangle shape doorway.) At the crown of our heads we connect with our 7th chakra, our connection to Source.  Breathe through the crown of your head and expand your 7th chakra into the heart of the Multiverse, All There Is, the Central Sun of all the Central Suns. Breathe in this expanded connection and then close the door to a perfect amount.

Perfection    Move down to the 6th chakra and allow the perfect connection to the Universe. Come back down to the Heart of the Galactic Mother (5th), down to the Heart of our Solar Angel (4th). Back to our Gaia connection (3rd), to our Lightbody (2nd) and all the way to the core of the Earth and our 1st chakra.

Enfold      From the first chakra enfold back and anchor into your 2nd chakra, your Lightbody and into your envelope of skin, feeling safe, grounded, vital and serene.

"Door Opening:

Love emerging,

life beckoning,

Miracles abounding,

life is so astounding,

Life unending,

On our knees bending"

in prayer, dedication and a connected Lightwork identity.

# Summary for Chapter 9

How do you like the SoulAnge Harmonic lineages? Have you worked with yours? Do you notice any difference?

_____

_____

_____

_____

_____

_____

_____

_____

What is your experience with the Expanded Chakra Meditation?

_____

_____

_____

_____

_____

_____

_____

_____

What is your present belief and understanding of the engine driving healing and energy work? Do you think quantum physics has anything to enrich your understanding? Have you read any quantum/ energy healing books?

_____

_____

_____

_____

_____

_____

_____

_____

_____

_____

_____

_____

_____

_____

_____

_____

Work with a few of the Quantum archetypes. Which one(s) are you guided to work with right now? What messages, wisdoms, or patterns are you receiving from working with them?

_____

_____

_____

_____

_____

_____

_____

_____

_____

_____

_____

_____

_____

_____

*The Universe is made of stories, not atoms*
*(Muriel Rukeyser)*

# Chapter 10

# Mudras

# and

# Mantras

# Section 31

## Our Song of Creation

'Mudras' are Sanskrit for 'gesture' or 'mark'. Mudras can be made with the entire body (think of Bollywood dances with stylized hand, head, arm, body, leg, and feet motions and rhythmic patterns). Most often, mudras are gestures made with the hand and fingers.

These sacred gestures open dimensional awareness within us as we focus upon an intent. Although fingers can be symbolic of elements and even planets in traditional yoga practice, for our Apprenticeship we will work with Lightworker intent and purpose.

'Mantras' are also from Sanskrit and they are sacred sounds, syllables, words, or phrases. These can be spoken, chanted, sung, or said silently, and form the basis of many prayers and invocations. 'Man' means 'mind' in Sanskrit and 'tra' means 'transport' or 'vehicle'. Thus, mantras are vehicles which transport us into a deeper mindset. Often, mantras are used in meditation and are vehicles to step us out of mind and into a larger, more expanded universal consciousness, rather than our linear 3D compartmentalizations.

Each month we will practice together on a combination mudra/mantra. Focusing together will enhance and heighten our work and make it easier for us to 'jump in' to the experience. Each day invest a few minutes of holding the mudra and stating the mantra. We will also work together during our group meeting to add to or expand our mantras until they feel right to us.

EnJoy this holistic, unique, yogic practice of mind/ body/ sacredness/ portal / transport!

# Month 1: Breathe and Connect

Mudra 1:      Non-dominant hand holds your field, about 8 inches from your body

On in-breath, with your dominant hand, touch thumb and forefinger together and bring hand down your body, following your breath from mouth to lower abdomen.

On outbreath palm open floats upwards from base of torso up and outwards

Do this procedure for 3 breaths

Mantra 1:      "I follow the swing of my eternal breath, the in-breath and out-breath of creation."

Mudra 2:      Hold both palms face up about shoulder height, breathing in the essence of being alive and being connected to All There Is.

Mantra 2:      "I connect with All There Is.

I am a Child of the Universe (feel relief and peace)

I am a Co-Creator of this Universe (feel empowered)

All is Well!"

1. What do you notice about your breath and connection?

_____

_____

_____

_____

_____

_____

_____

## Month 2: Protection

Mudra 1:   Draw Cho Ku Rei in front of you, on your field, about 12 inches in front of you. Motion your hands outwards to the right and left of your body, about 12 inches on each side. Motion your hands at the top of your head, about 12 inches above your head.

This is your personal energy field. It should feel boundaried, not shredded and not armored. It is egg shaped, luminous, and protectedly permeable to our environment and to All There Is.

Feel your personal space.

Mantra 1:   "I am safe. I am protected.

I am perfectly incarnated within my physical vehicle.

Thank you!"

Mudra 2:   Open and flick your hands and blow open your field, top, bottom and sides. Envision that you are blowing your field wider than normal 12 inches or so and you extend a few feet wider.

Any arrows or barbs thrown at you flow effortlessly through your field, and fall inertly to the ground behind you. Negativity from others or from stressful situations are unable to penetrate within you. Quantum physics tells us we are mostly made of 'empty' space. Therefore, we fashion a wider protective boundary.

Mantra 2:   "Archangel Michael, please help and shield me from negativity.

Light is all there is. Love is all there is."

2.  What do you notice about feeling protected?

_____

_____

_____

_____

_____

# Month 3: Surrender and Acceptance

Mudra 1:     Head bowed. Shoulders bowed. Non-dominant hand, close fist. Lightly tap heart center in 3 timed increments. Can also be on bended knee.

Mantra 1:     "Lord, have mercy upon my soul

Christ, have mercy upon my soul

Please, have mercy upon me"

Mudra 2:     Head bowed. Shoulders bowed. Hands folded at heart center with one palm on top of the other. Breathe.

Mantra 2:     (For another person's plight)

"I recognize you as a Being of Love and Light who has chosen, on a Soul level, this life path. I honor your free will choices."

(For your own plight)

"I am a Being of Love and Light. I always do the best I can at every moment. Please help me to accept that I am perfectly imperfect! Thank you for this precious life."

1. What do you notice about surrender and acceptance?

_____

_____

_____

_____

_____

_____

_____

_____

## Month 4: Building a Cone of Power

Mudra:

Stand with feet hip length apart. Bend slowly starting with your head to your chin, round your shoulders, mid back, lower back. Go as low as you feel comfortable, bending your knees, touching the Earth.

Slowly make your way back up, stacking your vertebrae slowly, straightening your shoulders, neck and finally head. Take 3 breaths. Feel the stability of your platform.

Bend the elbow of your non-dominant hand, palm facing up. Envision that you are receiving energy from Infinite Abundance.

With your dominant hand, move your hand in a clockwise circle, starting around your 3$^{rd}$ chakra, your solar plexus. Your hand is about 6 inches in front of your body. This is the seat of your power, control center, and identity.

Slowly raise the circle to your 4$^{th}$ chakra, your heart center. Widen the circle as you go upwards. Circle the area in front of your 5$^{th}$, 6$^{th}$, and 7$^{th}$ chakras.

The circle starts small and widens as you move upwards.

The circle starts slowly and gathers speed and power.

Blow as you build your cone of power.

Mantra:     "I now build my Cone of Power.

I bravely walk, step by step, onto my Highest Destiny Path.

Thank you for this opportunity!

I love you!"

4. What do you notice about your power center?

_____

_____

_____

_____

_____

_____

# Month 5: Focus

Mudra 1:    Sit comfortably on a chair, cushion, or floor. Arrange your legs so they are comfortable.

Fold your hands with fingers intertwined.

Have two index fingers straight out and touching at the tips. Have two thumbs straight out and touching at the tips. The two index fingers point away from you. The two thumbs point straight at your heart center.

Breathe. Focus.

Mantra 1:    "I am the point of stillness within the sea of creation.

I focus with single pointed intent upon that which is the heart of the matter."

Mudra 2:    Move your interlocked fingers out in front of your body a few inches. Pull your dominant hand back as if you were pulling the string of a bow and arrow. Your non-dominant arm is straight out, pointed directly at a target in the distance. What are you aiming at?

Draw your breath in slowly and consciously as you draw back your arrow. Blow out and release towards your target, releasing and flicking your fingers.

Mantra 2:    "I am precisely attuned to my cherished goal.

I always hit my mark."

5.   What do you notice about focus and attention?

_____

_____

_____

_____

_____

_____

_____

# Month 6: Increasing 'Clairs'

Mudra:      Stand, sit or lie comfortably. Put your hands on your heart center, palms one on top of the other. Take turns with your right hand touching your heart center and then your left hand touching your heart center with each mudra below. Feel the sensations. Take 3 conscious breaths.

Clairvoyance:    Bring your palms to a comfortable space about 6 inches in front of your eyes. Move your hands in a small circular motion outwards. Envision opening space in front of your eyes.

Mantra:      "I clearly see that only Love is real."

Clairaudience:   Bring your palms to a comfortable space about 6 inches to the sides of your ears. Move your hands in a small circular motion outwards. Envision opening space in your ears.

Mantra:      "I easily hear the frequencies of Love and Light."

Clairsentience:  Bring your palms to a comfortable space about 6 inches in front of your heart. Move your hands in a small circular motion outwards. Envision opening space in your heart.

Mantra:      "I open to the energies of All There Is. I receive heart based information easily and joyfully."

Overall Mantra: "I am a vibrational interpreter in a vibrational universe. I now claim my natural birthright as an intuitive."

6.  What do you notice about increasing your intuitive gifts?

_____

_____

_____

_____

_____

_____

_____

_____

_____

_____

_____

_____

_____

_____

_____

_____

_____

# Month 7: Increasing Perceptors of Healing

Mudra:     To increase perceptions when healing, use a clear quartz crystal or visualize using a clear quartz crystal or an etheric generator wand.

With your dominant index finger, touch each fingertip with crystal or wand on your non-dominant hand End with touching your palm. Visualize and intend that your receptors are heightening to pick up more subtle vibrations.

Repeat using non-dominant index finger for dominant hand.

Either touch the soles of your toes with a crystal or envision doing so. Wiggle each toe on one foot and then the other.

Using a crystal or envision touching a circle upon the top of your head, your crown chakra.

Mantra:     "I raise my perceptions. I heighten my receptors.

I am a vibrational interpreter of the highest and greatest.

So be it."

7.   What do you notice about your perceptions in healing?

_____

_____

_____

_____

_____

_____

_____

_____

# Month 8: Karuna, Compassionate Love

Mudra:    Stand with feet hip length apart. Bend slowly starting with your head to your chin, round your shoulders, mid back, lower back. Go as low as you feel comfortable, bending your knees, touching the Earth.

Slowly make your way back up, stacking your vertebrae slowly, straightening your shoulders, neck and finally head.

Begin to raise your arms up and out, as in a V position above your head. Raise your head. Look up envisioning the sun shining down on you. Breathe.

Mantra:    "I am filled with the light of the sun, our Solar Angel. I love you, sun. Thank you for your warmth!

Look straight ahead and lower your arms to shoulder length, pointing them straight to either side, palms facing outwards. Breathe.

Mantra:    "I beam love and acceptance to all, as the sun beams down on us all. I love you all! Thank you for your company on this journey."

Slowly bring arms folded at chest, crossing palms at heart center. Breathe.

Mantra:    "I beam undying love to myself. I love you now and forever!"

8.   What do you notice about your openness to love unconditionally?

_____

_____

_____

_____

_____

_____

_____

_____

## Month 9: Angel Wings

Mudra:       Put your right hand on your left shoulder and touch a few inches below the top. Flick your fingers upward. Put your left hand on your right shoulder and touch a few inches below the top. Flick your fingers upwards.

Raise both arms directly over your head and slowly motion them outwards and downwards, as if you were fluffing out your feathers.

Move your shoulder blades around a few times, feeling the weight of your opened and fluffed out wings.

Walk around a little, noticing the different gravitational pull as you have opened your wings.

Mantra:      "I am an eternal, powerful, majestic Spirit, incarnating in human form for my own pleasure and for the adventure and joy of it!"

9. What do you notice about walking around as an Angel?

_____

_____

_____

_____

_____

_____

_____

_____

_____

_____

_____

# Month 10: The Gift

Mudra:      Stand, sit or lie comfortably. Put your hands on your heart center, palms one on top of the other.

Call upon Beings of Love and Light to be with you.

Hold your open palms outward to receive a gift which is being given to you for your heart's desire. It could be for healing work, to increase abundance, to gain clarity, to release fear or blocks. There is an infinite supply of gifts which are available to us at all times for all reasons.

Open your arms to receive a gift today.

Mantra:     "Thank you for this gift!"

See or feel the gift. It can be a quality, a memory, an object, a feeling. It can change every day. You can ask for more information if you don't understand what the gift is.

"Thank you for (the specific gift)."

Mudra:      Start with your palms crossed, facing upwards, near your heart center. Open wide your arms.

Mantra:     "Please accept my gift!"

If you wish, give a specific gift to Spirit.

10.  What do you notice about this gift giving and receiving?

_____

_____

_____

_____

_____

_____

# Month 11: Lightning Rod of Connection and Transmission

Mudra:  Stand comfortably. Put your hands on your heart center, palms one on top of the other.

Call upon Beings of Love and Light to be with you.

Put your left hand out and upwards, with your left palm facing upwards. You are connecting with Source.

Put your right hand out and over the client's field with your right palm facing downwards. You are transmitting higher frequencies.

Breathe.

Accept the love and recognition for you and all your work from your entourage.

Mantra:  "I stand with this Beloved Being as Co-Creators, Thank you for this connection and transmission of healing, balance and empowerment."

11. What do you notice about your ability to connect and transmit your co-creator empowerment?

_____

_____

_____

_____

_____

_____

_____

_____

_____

# Month 12: Merkaba Eliahu, Lightbody

Mudra:        Sit comfortably. Put your hands on your heart center, palms one on top of the other.

Call upon Beings of Love and Light to be with you.

Call up a template of your Lightbody. Envision circles of light and connectors above your head, to the left and right sides, the front and back sides, the bottom of your feet and below, into the Earth.

With both of your index fingers, check your connections by lightly tracing sacred geometry shapes of triangles, circles, squares in your field. Trace Metatron's cube of 13 circles.

When you are connected in your Lightbody, consciously connect to global Lightworkers by motioning your fingers outwards.

Mantra:        "I connect with and send my Light to increase Love and Light on this precious planet and to all who live on her".

Consciously connect to the Grid of Lightworkers and Ascended Beings who are stationed above the planet by motioning your fingers upwards and outwards as if we are touching the stars.

Mantra:        "I connect with the Grid of Lightworkers and add my Light to increase Love and Light on this precious planet and to All There Is."

# Chapter 10 Summary

Have you enjoyed working with mudras?  What was a particular favorite of yours?

_____

_____

_____

_____

_____

_____

Have you enjoyed working with mantras? What was a particular favorite of yours?

_____

_____

_____

_____

_____

_____

_____

_____

_____

_____

_____

*True love is not for the fainthearted  (Meyer Baba)*

# Chapter 11

# Dedication

# and

# Service

# Shining Our Light!

As Lightworkers, Souls in Service, and Lighthouse energies, our job is to relax, breathe, vibrate at our highest, and shine our light! We can do this in a number of ways.

The most visible way of shining our light is to offer our energy healing services to others. Most people who train in Reiki or other energy fields are drawn like magnets to this field and either dearly long to do this work professionally or dearly long *not* to do this work on clients, ever.

It is up to you, your level of comfort in offering your services, and your destiny path. You certainly do not have to offer healing sessions. But, you might want to send Reiki to yourself, to loved ones or to our global situations. That is shining our light.

Perhaps you might only want to offer energy classes, give workshops, or write about these experiences. This is also shining our light. There is no right way to shine our light.

Keeping ourselves clear, balanced, hopeful, and, maybe even joyful is a wonderful dedication and service. You have many tools to center and align yourself every day. Perhaps align with every breath? It's a great goal!

From that balanced and connected perspective, and as a soul-in-service, as you feel the connection and joy, you vibrate accordingly, and you change the world!

For those who wish to publicly step forth and shine for others, Chapter 11 discusses relevant topics to professionalize yourself. Section 32 offers multiple ways to broadcast your work and we end with Section 33 and the prayer of the Bodhisattva, Peace Prayer of St. Francis, and the Post Apprentice Check-In.

We have come this far, let's see this through to the end!

# Section 32

## Broadcasting Your Unique Vibration

Bringing your work out to the world is a wonderful gift! YOU are a wonderful gift! At this time, it still is difficult to make a living as an energy healer, although some do. Recommendations would be to start slowly, build a practice, and add other offerings as well.

Following are business steps:

1. Inner clarity
2. 'Advisory Board'
3. 'Prayer of Intent' for stepping forward
4. Affirmations
5. Design a name and logo
6. Network, network, network
7. Decide upon place of service
8. Protections, conditions, portals of Light
9. Insurance coverage
10. Advertising
11. Social media
12. Sales Force'
13. Aesthetics and ambience
14. Exchange of energy
15. Gratitude
16. Confidentiality
17. Going public
18. Highest Destiny Path
19. Offering Classes
20. Manuals and certificates
21. Believe in yourself!
22. EnJoy It All!

## Bring 'Inner Clarity' to your process

Begin with yourself. Reflect upon your heart's desire, your availability, and your destiny path. Vision your final product. Vision yourself doing this work. Ask for guidance in this process

## Call upon an 'Advisory Board'

Set an intent and verbally call upon your personal 'Advisory Board' to help you move forward and offer your services to others. Call upon those Beings of Love and Light you align with, and then extend the invitation to other Beings of Love and Light who wish to align with you and your purpose. Spend time meditating and receiving information from this board. Every day, ask, "What is it I need to do today?"

## Make a 'Prayer of Intent' for stepping forward

Create your own Prayer of Intent. Add a personal mudra or mantra. EnJoy saying this prayer every day, keeping your focus on the Highest and Greatest Good for all. Remember in the universal Law of Attraction, we ask, the universe answers, we receive and vibrate to the level of accepting the answer. Often, time is involved. Often, more clarity is needed. Often, the answer appears in a different way than we expected.

## Affirmations

"Like unto itself is drawn." That is the universal law of attraction. Affirm ease and effortlessness in stepping forward. Affirm that you are guided. Ask every day what it is you need to know and to do today. Listen for an upwelling message from within. Then affirm that message to yourself during the day.

Be careful not to add negative language to your affirmation or future tense (do not say, "I will get …. clients" because 'will' gives a message to your subconscious that it will not be 'today' but in the future).

## Design a name and logo

Have fun designing your brand! What colors are you drawn to? What images? Are you specializing in a certain population (example, women) or a certain issue (example, stress relief)? Design business cards, simple flyers or brochure.

## Network, network, network

Gain courage and speak to others about your new business. Talk to friends, neighbors, even family. Networking is still the number 1 way to get clients.

## Decide upon place of service

We are fortunate that we can do our work in any number of places. Invest in a Reiki or massage table, a massage chair, and basic supplies like sheets, neck pillow, and leg pillow. Where will you offer your services?

At home? Check for easy entrance to your space, and accessibility to a restroom. Phones, animals, cooking scents, and other people – all distractions need to be taken into account. It is hard to bring people into your home, especially if they need to move through your personal space.  This option precludes advertising and bringing strangers in your home.

Rent an office space? This costs a larger outlay of finances before you will offset this with services. Perhaps you can share with others? You can depend upon Spirit to help bring customers, but you will also need to have a good advertising strategy and foundational support.

## Protections, conditions, portals of Light

Set protections around your space. Draw Cho Ku Rei's on the ceilings, the 4 walls, above and below your head.  Call upon the Beings of Love and Light to protect you, your space, your clients.

Open portals of light so that clients are drawn to you. Visualize golden invitations being given to those who resonate with you and who would benefit from your work.

### Insurance coverage

The International Center for Reiki Training, directed by William Rand, offers insurance for Reiki practitioners. You must first register as a member which has an annual fee of approximately $150. Then you are eligible for Reiki insurance, which has an annual fee of approximately $150. There is a $1,000,000 coverage protection. If you are going to be seeing clients and not just family and friends, then I strongly recommend you get insurance coverage.

### Advertising

There are many ways to advertise your business. The best ways I have found are to offer workshops, classes, and Reiki Circles. Consider designing a website, even a simple one page site. Although business is not as driven by websites anymore in my experience, still it presents you as a professional and viable offering. Business cards do as well.

## Social Media

Social media is crucial for reaching out to others. Facebook is important, not just a personal page, but a business one as well. Email is not as crucial as it once was, but, again, sending out information or newsletters is a great way to express yourself and to reach others. Instagram, Twitter, LinkedIn, are all good ways to develop your client base.

## 'Sales Force'

As with your 'Advisory Board', creating your own Beings of Love and Light 'Sales Force' is a great addition. I often run my schedule through my 'Sales Force' letting them know when I would like additional clients, and asking their help for re-scheduling when I need some down time.

## Aesthetics and ambience

This is the fun part – bringing your personality and your design sense to your healing space. Be mindful of your population, though. What is the underlying message you want to give? Strike a balance between your inspiration and the inward comfort of those who come in.

## Exchange of energies

There needs to be an exchange of energies that honors both the client's needs and your time investment. Money is the cleanest form of exchange in our society. However, for most people it is awkward and uncomfortable to ask for and receive money from family and close friends. Consider an exchange of barter. If that is not feasible, then consider their giving you feedback, perhaps immediately and in a few days' time, which can give you insight into your work with them.

A final step removed, which is taking you out of the equation completely, is to ask them to say prayers or visualize light around a situation. For example, if they came for knee problems, then perhaps they could pray for those who are facing amputation or knee surgery. In this way, there is an exchange of energy, although it is to our global community and not to you personally.

## Gratitude

Express gratitude every day, even if you have one client for feedback exchange, feel the gratitude of shining your light and doing your work. No clients today? Then spend your time practicing your craft, sending to others, meditating, channeling, writing, journaling, creating and being grateful for this prep time and down time. Vision what it is you want – the type of client, your business hours, how busy you wish to be, your outreach in the community. And be grateful for it all. You are sending to the Light Grid so that another person can benefit from your visions and light markers. Their business success links back to you.

## Confidentiality

We can hear or interpret personal information for our clients during a session. This needs to be respected and you should assure your clients that what transpires in the session is held in strict confidentiality by you.

## Going public

One good way of going public is by offering Reiki Circles, either free or for a donation. Your investment of time, expertise, and healing work is expanded by developing a group of people who enjoy coming for Reiki. This is a wonderful group energy that can build over time. It is also a good group of people who would want to train with you one day.

## Highest Destiny Path

You can walk the path that you are standing upon, but is it your Highest and Greatest Destiny Path? Have you set the affirmation that you intend to walk you highest destiny path? Once you do, still your mind and see what pops up from the depths within you. Are you concerned that your family and friends might not understand or support you? Are you concerned you won't make enough money? Are you concerned about stepping forward publicly? Are you concerned that you are not in a good enough space to 'deserve' this work? There are many reasons, some sabotaging, some just in need of clean-up, that arise when we intend to walk our Highest Destiny Path.

## *Classes*

Offering to train others in Reiki is a wonderful addition to your practice. You are able to empower others to step forward to heal themselves and others in their lives, rather than have people continue to come see you. To teach, you must be attuned at the Reiki Master level. As a Lightworker, you are definitely able to step forward to Reiki Master level and beyond into advanced energy healing techniques.

Start by offering and attuning client to Reiki 1, then build up to Reiki 2. You might also start by attuning one person, and, after you begin to feel comfortable with the trainings, you can add multiple people in the class. Ask your 'Training Angels' for help in getting students to train. Visualize yourself doing this work. Practice giving attunements on stuffed animals. Practice your Prayer of Intent and Guided Visualizations. It is a wonderful service to attune others into the sacred Reiki healing work.

## *Manuals and certificates*

For classes you will need manuals and certificates. Books 6 and 7 of the Tools for Lightworkers Series is the Reiki 1, 2 and Reiki Master Manuals. The International Center for Reiki Training sells William Rand's two manuals, The Healing Touch: Reiki First and Second Degree Manual and Reiki Master Manual. There are also manuals available at bookstores and online.

Students also need you to certify them after their classes. These certifications are required to participate in community healing events. Keep a detailed record of each class and student so that you may reproduce certificates years later if need be.

## *Believe in yourself!*

Believe in your ability to manifest your energy healing practice! If it gets off to a slow start, so what? It does not 'mean' that you are not good for this work or that it won't happen for you. The world needs you to vibrate at your highest. The world needs you to walk your highest destiny path, whatever that might be. Hold no agendas about the particulars, just rejoice in the moment by moment brightness.

## *EnJoy it All!*

Above all, enJoy this precious life and this sacred experience!

# Section 33

## *Shantideva, The Bodhisattva Vows*

*May I be a guard for those who need protection*

*A guide for those on the path*

*A boat, a raft, a bridge for those who wish to cross the flood*

*May I be a lamp in the darkness*

*A resting place for the weary*

*A healing medicine for all who are sick*

*A vase of plenty, a tree of miracles*

*And for the boundless multitudes of living beings*

*May I bring sustenance and awakening*

*Enduring like the earth and sky*

*Until all beings are freed from sorrow*

*And all are awakened.*

## Peace Prayer of St. Francis

*Lord, make me an instrument of your peace.*

*Where there is hatred, let me sow love;*
*where there is injury, pardon;*
*where there is doubt, faith;*
*where there is despair, hope;*
*where there is darkness, light;*
*where there is sadness, joy.*

*O divine Master, grant that I may not so much seek*
*to be consoled as to console,*
*to be understood as to understand,*

*to be loved as to love.*

*For it is in giving that we receive,*
*it is in pardoning that we are pardoned,*
*and it is in dying that we are born to eternal life.*

*Amen.*

# Summary Chapter 11

What is a good Prayer of Intent for starting your business?

_____

_____

_____

_____

_____

_____

_____

_____

_____

_____

_____

_____

_____

_____

_____

_____

_____

Did you create your 'Board of Advisors' and 'Sales Force'? Who are some of the 'Participants'?

_____

_____

_____

_____

_____

Do you have a name you would like to call your business?  Colors? Logo?

_____

_____

_____

_____

Visualize yourself at your business, your perfect location, doing the work you love. What would that be?

_____

_____

_____

_____

_____

_____

*Immaculate Perfection! (Prem Rawat)*

# Post-Apprentice Check-In

The following check-in will help you gauge your pre-Apprentice understandings. Review your Pre-Apprentice Check-In which you filled out in the beginning of this training. What surprises and reflections are you noticing?

Date:_____

Do you identify yourself as a Lightworker?

_____

_____

Do you identify yourself as an Energy Worker?

_____

_____

How else do you identify yourself?

_____

_____

What does it mean to be a Lightworker?

_____

_____

_____

_____

_____

_____

Did you get what you wanted from this Apprenticeship?

_____

_____

_____

_____

_____

_____

Are you happy with your daily alignment? Anything you would like to be different?

_____

_____

_____

_____

_____

What are some of your self-care tools?

_____

_____

_____

_____

_____

_____

_____

Do you send energy every day for the Highest and Greatest Good for situations?

_____

_____

_____

Do you have intuitive gifts?  Please explain...

_____

_____

_____

_____

_____

_____

_____

_____

_____

What is the highest vision you hold for yourself?

_____

_____

_____

_____

_____

_____

Do you have more belief in yourself as a healer and Lightworker?

_____

_____

_____

_____

_____

_____

_____

_____

Do you feel comfortable calling upon your Lightworker Community?

_____

_____

_____

_____

_____

_____

_____

_____

_____

What goals have you met and what goals do you still hold now?

_____

_____

_____

_____

_____

_____

_____

_____

_____

_____

_____

_____

_____

_____

_____

_____

_____

*It is an honor and a joy to walk this path with you!*

*Thank you for your commitment, dedication, and for shining your unique and precious Light for us to see more clearly*

*through the fog of 3D*

*into the meta-dimensional prism*

*of love and light!*

*Blessings and Hugs!*

*Lorelynn*

# *About the Author*

## Lorelynn Mirage Cardo, PhD

After following the traditional paths of obtaining a masters and doctoral degree in counseling and education, I followed my heart into the realm of energy healing including Reiki, Integrated Etheric Healing, and quantum healing techniques.

If you are guided to work with me, trust that you are a Lightworker and a Soul in Service!

Through the Arise School of Healing Arts I have incorporated an Apprenticeship Program so those interested in learning or advancing their healing arts skills can do so within a personal and loving environment, through individual and small group sessions. Trainings range from introductory through advanced levels including methods which have originated through Arise.

Although I still have my Queens and Long Island, NY accent, I have been living in Portland, Oregon for the last twenty years with my sweet family, Tony, Bethany our daughter, our adorable Mia (a rescue poodle mix) and Elijah, our brave and wondrous cat. All of my animals (11) have loved to get Reiki, and my cats love to jump up on the massage table and give Reiki as well! Come visit if you are in the area. And, as time and distance are not obstacles in our field, connect if you feel guided!

The *Tools for Lightworkers* series is written just for you, from my heart to yours. Let's work together as Lightworkers, shining our light during these shifting times! Feel free to keep in touch- you can reach me at www.AriseGuide.com or Lorelynn@AriseGuide.com.

I send Love and Light everyday so contact me anytime. Love to you! EnJOY!

# Acknowledgements

I am so grateful to share this Lightworker Orientation and Training Manual with you!

I wish to acknowledge Tony, Bethany, and Parker – my lifelines! You are my inspiration and my hope!

Thanks, Kristen Broten, for the wonderful Lightworker graphic and for the cover design! I love doing this series with you! Thanks also to Marni Derr, Chris Duncan and Cue Raven Publishing. You're the best! Special thanks to Bethany for her editing help in the middle of wedding prep and medical school. Thanks also to Mariana Ruzsak for her inspiring Angel Tree design.

Love and appreciation to all my family, especially Che and Linda. Dolorese, Larry, Barbara. Walter. Carol, Betty, Veronica, Kay – so many wonderful women who have shared their stories, strengths, and lives with me. To my wonderful nieces and nephews – I love you all!

Much gratitude and love to all my clients, students and friends throughout the years – I have written this book and the entire *Tools for Lightworkers* series for you!

I especially am grateful and honored to journey with the Amazing Arise Apprentices – Alex Mazziotti, Amy Burns, Annie Bishop, Beth Vanderzee, Candy Crippen, Diane Holt, Felicia Christensen, Heidi Fuiten, Hillary and Bella Darling, Jeff Luster, Jodi Gartman, Kayleigh Farris, Kimberly Armstrong, Kristin Broten, Loraine Weers, Merrill Watts, Michelle Collins, Norah Zaharakis, and Tyleena Winslow! Your lights shine forth!!

Thanks also to Kimberly and her expansive Turtles Yoga and Wellness!

In keeping with our *GRACE!* process, I also humbly acknowledge so many luminaries who have inspired me:

Ground:  Gaia, Paramahansa Yogananda, Turtles

Root:  Walter, Marie, Ann, Mary, Vincent, John Lennon, Martin Luther King Jr.

Align:  Lee Carroll and Kryon, Jule Kowarsky, Asandra Lamb

Center:  Austin Angel, Esther Hicks and Abraham, my beloved companion animals

Elevate:  Prem Rawat, Hafiz, Daniel Ladinsky, Angels & heavenly songs, Beings of Love and Light

Alchemical Pop!  Elorhaim Seraphim Magnificat energies, Oriel, SoulAnge & Arise Architects

And dedicated to Lightworkers everywhere and everywhen, shining Light in the darkness. For You!

# References

Adorney, John feat. Daya. *Beckoning*. Eversound CD, 1998.

Anderson, Brenda. *Playing the Quantum Field*. Novato, CA: New World Library, 2006.

Barks, Coleman, translation. *The Essential Rumi*. San Francisco, CA: HarperCollins, 1995.

Bohm, Niels. *Wholeness and the Implicate Order*. London: Routledge Classics, 1980.

Bolen, Jean Shinoda. *Goddesses in Everywoman*, NY: Harper Collins, 1984.

Bolen, Jean Shinoda. *Goddesses in Older Women*. NY: Harper Collins, 2001.

Bolen, Jean Shinoda. *Gods in Everyman*. NY: Harper and Row, 1989.

Braden, Gregg. *The Spontaneous Healing of Belief*. NY: Hay House, 2008.

Braden, Gregg. *The Science of Miracles*, NY: Hay House, 2009.

Braden, Gregg. *Fractal Time*. NY: Hay House, 2010.

Braden, Gregg. *The Turning Point*. NY: Hay House. 2014.

Campbell, Joseph. *The Power of Myth*. NY: Anchor Books, 1988.

Clow, Barbara Hand. *Alchemy of 9 Dimensions*. Charlottesville, VA: Hampton Roads Press, 2004.

Davis, Elizabeth and Leonard, Carole. The *Woman's Wheel of Life*. NY: Viking Penguin, 1996.

De Chardin, Pierre. *The Phenomenon of Man*. Toronto, CAN: The Great Library R.P. Pryne, 2015.

d'Espagnat, Bernard. *On Physics and Philosophy*. Princeton, NJ: Princeton U. Press, 2006.

Ford, Kenneth. *The Quantum World*. NY: First Harvard University Press, 2006.

Gaia, Laurelle Shanti. *The Book on Karuna Reiki*. Hartsel, CO: Infinite Light Healing, 2001.

*Gimbutas, Marija. The Languge of the Goddess*. London: Thames and Hudson, 1989.

Grout, Pam. *E Squared*. NY: Hay House, 2013.

Halpern, Steven. *Chakra Suite*. Seven Halpern's Inner Peace Music, 2003.

Hawkins, David. *Transcending the Levels of Consciousness*. NY: Hay House, 2006.

Hicks, Esther and Hicks, Jerry. *Ask and It Is Given*. NYC: Hay House, 2004

Hicks, Esther and Hicks, Jerry. *The Vortex*. NY: Hay House, 2009.

Jung, Carl. *Man and His Symbols*. Aldus Books. London. 1964.

Katz, Michael. *Wisdom of the Gemstone Guardians*. Portland, OR: Natural Healing Press, 2004.

Kryon and Muranyi, Monika. *The Gaia Effect*. Quebec, CAN: Ariane Books, 2013

Kryon and Muranyi, Monika. *The Human Akash*. Quebec, CAN: Ariane Books, 2014.

Kryon and Muranyi, Monika. *The Human Soul Revealed*. Quebec, CAN: Ariane Books, 2015.

Kryon. *The Recalibration of Humanity*. San Diego, CA: The Kryon Writings Inc., 2013

Kryon. *The Twelve Layers of DNA*. CA: The Platinum Publishing Co., 2010

Ladinsky, Daniel, ed. *I Heard God Laughing: Renderings of Hafiz*. NY: Penguin Compass, 2006.

Ladinsky, Daniel, ed. *The Subject Tonight Is Love: Hafiz*. NY: Penguin Compass, 2003.

Ladinsky, Daniel, ed. *The Gift: Poems by Hafiz* NY: Penguin Press, 1999.

Ladinsky, Daniel, ed. *Love Poems from God : Twelve Sacred Voices from the East and West*. NY: Penguin Compass, 2002.

Ladinsky, Daniel, ed. *A Year With Hafiz: Daily Contemplations*. NY: Penguin Compass. 2010.

Ladinsky, Daniel, ed. *The Purity of Desire: 100 Poems of Rumi*. NY: Penguin Books. 2012.

Maslow, Abraham. *Toward a Psychology of Being*. Floyd, VA: Sublime Books, 2014.
Myss, Carolyn. *Sacred Contracts*. NY: Three Rivers Press: 2002.

Newton, Michael. *Destiny of Souls*. St. Paul, MN: Llewellyn, 2001.

Newton, Michael. *Life Between Lives*. St. Paul, MN: Llewellyn, 2004.

Newton, Michael. *Journey of Souls*. St. Paul, MN: Llewellyn, 1994.

Pert, Candace. *Molecules of Emotion: The Science Behind Mind-Body Medicine*. NY: Touchstone, 1999.

Pierce, John Randolph. *The Abundance Book*. NY: Hay House, 1987.

Premal, Deva and DeLory, Donna. *Songs of Kuan Yin*. Sounds True CD Pub, 2010.

Radin, Dean. *Science, Yoga, and the Evidence for Extraordinary Psychic Abiliites*. NY: Deepak Chopra Books, 2013.

Radin, Dean. *The Conscious Universe*. NY: Deepak Chopra Books, 2009.

Rand, William. *The Healing Touch: Reiki First and Second Degree Manual* . Southfield, MI: Vision Pub., 1991.

Reid, Natalie. *5 Steps to a Quantum Life*. Bozeman, MT: Winged Horse Publishing, 2007.

Rosenblum, Bruce and Kuttner, Fred. *Quantum Enigma: Physics Encounters Consciousness*. NY: Oxford University Press, 2011.

Sheldrake, Rupert. *Science Set Free*. NY: Deepak Chopra Books, 2012.

Sheldrake, Rupert. *The Sense of Being Stared At*. Rochester, Vermont: Park Street Press. 2013.

Starhawk. *The Spiral Dance*. NY: Harper 1979.

Stone, Merlin. *Ancient Mirrors of Womanhood*. NY: Harcourt Pub., 1979.

Stone, Merlin. *When God Was A Woman*, NY: Harcourt Pub., 1976.


www. Abraham-Hicks.com

www. DoTerra. Com

www. Fesflowers. Com

www. Gemisphere.com

www. Kryon.com

www. Perelandra-ltd. com

www. Timeless today.com

www. Youngliving.com